V FOR VENDETTA

ALAN MOORE
DAVID LLOYD

WITH STEVE WHITAKER AND SIOBHAN DODDS

"I'd never really been interested in having my work adapted for film. So I decided that the only thing that I could do that would be taking the high ground on the issue would be to refuse any future payments for films that were made of my work. "

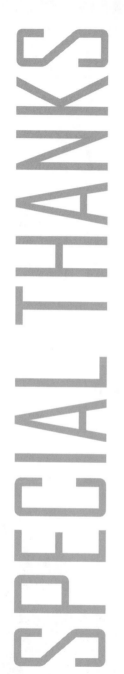

SPECIAL THANKS

The author would like thank . . .

Alan Moore for his generosity of spirit, abiding patience and continued support throughout the long process of seeing our latest conversation into print.

I believe that makes two pints I owe you, mate.

José Villarrubia for the use of yet another one of his wonderful photos for this book's cover, and his continued support and friendship.

That's two I owe you, as well, my friend!

Rich Maurizio for publishing the Bill Baker Presents... books. And for putting up with my particular brand of lunacy–for yet another year, no less.

Paul Michael Kane for just getting it–utterly and completely–as a designer, as a webmaster and as a friend.

Chris Staros, Brent Warnock and **Top Shelf** because it's an incredible company run by some really wonderful folks. And, this particular time out, for having the guts, the heart, and the determination to publish Lost Girls ... and for having the vision and courage to do it right the first time. Bravo!

A veritable **host of other people**–literally too many to name here–including those creators, publishers and support personnel, the fans, my fellow journalists and all the other good folks I've met and spoken with over the years, whether on or off the record, each of whom has helped me better my work in ways both large and small.

And finally, you, the reader, for picking up this book, opening the pages and making it all real again. Even if only for a second...

Because, without each of you, none of this would have been possible, nor mean as much.

**Bill Baker
at the BFD Studios, 2007**

Illustration Credits:

Cover   José Villarrubia, photo of Alan Moore (© 2005 José Villarrubia).

page 3   Alan Moore, David Lloyd, et. al., V for Vendetta trade paperback (© DC Comics) dust jacket illustration, Science Fiction Book Club hardcover, DC Comics, 1987.

page 6   Bill Baker and Alan Moore, Alan Moore Spells It Out (text © 2005 William M. S. Baker, photo © 2005 José Villarrubia, and is used with the kind permission of Top Shelf Productions) cover illustration, Airwave Publishing, 2005.

page 7   Bill Baker, photo (© 2006 William M. S. Baker).

page 8   Alan Moore, et. al., ABC Sketchbook (© America's Best Comics, LLC) cover illustration, America's Best Comics, LLC, 2002.

page 15   Alan Moore, Dave Gibbons, et. al., Watchmen trade paperback (© DC Comics) cover illustration, DC Comics, 1987.

page 21   Alan Moore and Eddie Campbell, A Disease of Language (© 2005 Alan Moore and Eddie Campbell) the final image of Snakes and Ladders from page 105, Knockabout-Palmano Bennett, 2005.

page 29   Alan Moore, Kevin O'Neill, et. al., The League of Extraordinary Gentlemen Vol. 1 (™ and © 1999-2006 Alan Moore and Kevin O'Neill) "My Message to Our Readers" page, America's Best Comics, LLC, 2000.

page 35   Alan Moore, et. al., DC Universe: The Stories of Alan Moore (© DC Comics) cover illustration by Brian Bolland, DC Comics, 2006.

page 41   Alan Moore, Rick Veitch, John Totleben, et. al., Swamp Thing # 37 (© DC Comics) cover illustration, DC Comics, June, 1985.

page 49   Alan Moore and Melinda Gebbie, Lost Girls Book 1 (© 1991-2006 Alan Moore and Melinda Gebbie) final panel of page 6, Chapter 1, Top Shelf Productions, August, 2006.

page 59   Alan Moore, Gary Leach, Alan Davis, Mick Anglo, et. al., Miracleman # 1 (© Neil Gaiman, Mark Buckingham, Mick Anglo, et. al.) cover illustration, Eclipse Comics, August, 1985.

page 71   Alan Moore, J. H. Williams III, Mick Gray, et. al., Promethea # 32 (© America's Best Comics, LLC) cover illustration, America's Best Comics, LLC, April, 2005.

page 80   José Villarrubia, photo of Alan Moore (© 2005 José Villarrubia) Bill Baker, self portrait (© 2006 William M. S. Baker)

back cover   Alan Moore and Eddie Campbell, A Disease of Language (© 2005 Alan Moore and Eddie Campbell) cover illustration, Knockabout-Palmano Bennett, 2005.

Alan Moore, Voice of the Fire (text © 1996-2003 Alan Moore, photo © 2003 José Villarrubia) dust jacket illustration, Top Shelf Productions, 2003.

Alan Moore and José Villarrubia, Mirror of Love (text © 1994-2004 Alan Moore, photos © 2004 José Villarrubia), dust jacket illustration, Top Shelf Productions, 2004.

Alan Moore and Melinda Gebbie, Lost Girls (© 1991-2006 Alan Moore and Melinda Gebbie) slipcase illustration, Top Shelf Productions, August, 2006.

About the Bill Baker Presents...series of books:

Alan Moore's Exit Interview is the second volume of the Bill Baker Presents... series of books. Each installment of this series features an in-depth interview with the best and the brightest, the rising stars and the living legends, the pioneers and the unsung workhorses from the comic book and other Pop Culture industries.

The inaugural release of the series, *Alan Moore Spells It Out* (2005), sold out of its initial print run in seven months. A second edition is in the planning stages at this time.

The third book in the Bill Baker Presents... series, *George Perez: The Best of All Worlds*, will be released in 2007.

A few words before we begin...

INTRODUCTION

For those first time readers who might be wondering if any foreknowledge of **Alan Moore Spells It Out** [the first installment in the Bill Baker Presents... series of extended interviews] is necessary to fully enjoy and understand this book, the honest answer is, "No, not really." All one really needs to know about our previous conversation is that, while it mainly concerned itself with Alan's ideas on magic, creativity and making comics, it also touched briefly upon some of the business-related concerns which have impinged upon that worthy's life-long pursuit of his muse--and that those same difficulties were major

Alan Moore Spells It Out, the first installment in the Bill Baker Presents... series of extended interviews.

© 2005 José Villarrubia

contributors to his decision to effectively end his involvement with commercial comics by entering into a self-imposed semi-retirement of sorts. Fortunately, all of these topics, as well as many others which were not previously addressed or perhaps had not even existed at that time, are covered in some detail within these pages as part of Moore's extended dissection of his own career.

For those who are familiar with that first book and were wondering, well, "Yes, this can be read as a direct sequel to Alan Moore Spells It Out." Still, this latest excerpt of my ongoing conversation with Alan marks something of a departure from the general tenor of my work, which has typically focused on the creative life of my subjects. Yes, it's true that Moore talks about, among other topics of creative import, his move towards writing directly at his computer, rather than first working in longhand before transcribing it to the computer as he's done in the past. Still, much of this volume is taken up with Alan's detailed examination of his quarter century spent working in commercial comics, and with his critique of the mainstream comic book industry and its sometimes questionable business practices and labor relations, leaving less time for more creative concerns.

Which leads nicely to my final comment on what follows, one intended mainly for those who might otherwise choose to interpret Moore's critique, and this book which presents it, as an attack upon the commercial comics industry in general, an attack upon any particular company, or even as an effort to embarrass or discredit any specific individuals who might work in the business. Quite simply, none of that interests me in the least.

My primary purpose here is historical. Specifically, to accurately capture and present Alan Moore's thoughts concerning his personal experiences while plying his trade in the funny book business. The fact that much of what Alan relates is, by turns, absolutely inspiring and utterly infuriating, incredibly funny and terribly painful, is not the point of this exercise. Or, at least, it's not the whole point. Alan deserves to have his say, it's true. But, as Moore himself intimates, there are larger issues at work here.

Ultimately, I hope that, by openly addressing the many real and vital concerns that Alan raises over the course of our conversation, this book will help others working in the business to avoid those errors of judgment and ethical lapses which have tripped up and frustrated him over the years...and which have bedeviled so many other creators and purveyors of comics, past and present. And while I realize that it's probably impossible to totally eliminate their existence, I still feel that it's important to try and help those generations of good folks who will follow to sidestep those same onerous pitfalls in the future.

At least, that's the impulse which gave rise to this book, and which has informed my own career as a comics journalist. My hopes for an improved medium—one which could also help realize the dream of a better, fairer and more fulfilling creative working life for artists in the future—remain alloyed with an enduring belief in the inherent and true worthiness of both the comics medium and those who labor in it.

And so it's with those twin goals firmly in mind, to better the art form and enrich the lives of those who literally live to make comics, that I offer Alan Moore's Exit Interview to you, the reader. Regardless of what you might seek from it, regardless of where the pursuit of your own dreams and hopes might take you, may it entertain and serve you well—today, tomorrow and always.

Bill Baker is a veteran entertainment and comics journalist, and the author of one other nonfiction book, *Alan Moore Spells It Out.*

Bill Baker
from the BFD Studios, somewhere in the wilds of Michigan's Upper Peninsula, USA
December, 2006

Alan Moore's
Exit Interview

Bill Baker: When we last spoke, you were planning a graceful exit from your commercial comics career, and entering into a sort of semi-retirement. However, things didn't quite go as planned, did they?

Alan Moore: Yeah. Well, as it happened, that is exactly what I did, although it was considerably more ugly and violent and final than I had expected it to be--or wished it be, quite frankly. But, as far as I can remember, the last time we were talking I was planning to finish off all of the various ABC books and then carry on *The League of Extraordinary Gentlemen* alone—well, just me and Kevin [O'Neill]. That would be the only book that I would be carrying on. And, at that time, I think that I was still quite happy with the idea of it being published by ABC.

BB: Correct.

AM: So, to recap the situation as it was then, I'd informed DC Comics through WildStorm, through ABC, that once I'd concluded all of the other ABC books to my satisfaction, then the only slender thread that would be connecting me with DC Comics would be *The League of Extraordinary Gentlemen*, which Kevin and I are lucky enough to own. And I made it clear that, because I'd been happy with the way that ABC had produced the previous two League volumes, I would be happy to continue to leave it like that, because I was happy with the job that ABC was doing.

On the other hand, as I also pointed out, ABC were ultimately owned by DC Comics, who were people that I was famously unhappy about working for. So, what I said to Scott Dunbier at the time was that I would be happy to continue with the future volumes of the League being published by ABC, just as long as the thing was done in a manner which didn't remind me that these things were being published by DC Comics.

No more sudden pulpings, no more attempts at editorial interference. I also stated that anything that happened that was like that, where I was made aware of the fact that it was ultimately DC Comics who were running the show, then I would be taking the title to another publisher and that that would be a final severance between me and DC Comics.

Scott assured me that he'd passed that message on to DC, as I believe he had done, and that they said that they were more than happy with that, that there certainly wouldn't be any interference, and that things could continue calmly and quietly as they had been.

It was around about this time that I ran into some problems with the film industry. This probably needs a little bit of a recap as to my previous dealings with the film industry, and the state of my relationship with them as it was at that time.

Now, ever since I started to do work that attracted interest from the film industry, which was pretty close to the beginning of my career, actually, I had taken a rather dim view of it. Possibly because my first exposure to having my work filmed was when they made the regrettable Return of the Swamp Thing which, due to the perhaps unwise contract that DC had signed with the producers of The Swamp Thing movie, back when DC were desperate to get any of their books filmed, the contract stated that the filmmakers were at liberty to take anything from The Swamp Thing title, from any point during the book's past or future.

That was why the second Swamp Thing film featured ideas and lines of butchered dialogue that had been taken from my comparatively thoughtful comics, making them travesties of my work, basically, which I wasn't too happy about. And I kind of decided at that point that things that were meant to be read as comic books probably didn't translate into films that well. This was just my personal opinion.

And then people started to talk about options for *Watchmen* and *V for*

Vendetta, which by that point I had realized that I had no say in, because they were owned by DC Comics, both of those titles. So, whether they got made into films or not was a thing that wasn't within my control.

But when it was suggested, I think, in both instances, I said that, frankly, I didn't think that they would make very good films, and that, certainly, they wouldn't be as good as the comic books.

It is my strong feeling that most adaptations are a bad idea. If something works well in the medium that it was intended for, why is there any reason to assume that it will work as well, or better, in an entirely different medium? It seems to me that the only motivation for these things can be that of making money by turning what might have been an earnest piece of work into a franchise that can be spun out into a series of films, and perhaps a series of products, or computer games–which has got nothing to do with the reason why I wrote the work in the first place.

So, that was my position; that I couldn't stop these films being made. I didn't think they were a very good idea. But, I was prepared to take the money. If they were going to make these things of mine into films, then I would take the money that I was being offered for them. This was largely because, at that point, I was living in a fool's paradise where–with the exception of The Swamp Thing film, which I wasn't offered any money for–none of my work had actually made it to the screen.

At that point, the procedure, as far as I could see, was that my work would be optioned. I would get, and the artist would get, a couple of chunky option payments, and then–best possible result–the film wouldn't get made. So we'd get this film money that people are being kind enough to give to us, and wouldn't have to sit through a botched end result. Now, this was working fine as a plan right up until *From Hell*, which was the first one of my books to actually get filmed, where it actually went into production.

Now, I was a bit surprised by this, but I decided that, "Okay, the film's going into production. The fairest thing for me to do is to simply keep my distance from it, to not be involved with the filming in any way, since the film was actually nothing that I was really interested in." And that was said with no disrespect to any of the parties involved in it. It was simply that I'd never really been interested in having my work made into a film. Also, the fact is that I would probably be the worst judge of any such film.

I am very picky about my writing, and one of the reasons I've worked in comics is because, in comics, every full-stop and every comma that I put in there will be on the finished page. I have complete control of how my work is presented.

In films that is not the case. I understood that, in order to make a film of a 600-page book like *From Hell*, then, obviously, there were going to have to be a lot of changes made. And while I understood that, as I have said from the very beginning of all this, if people are going to have to butcher my children, effectively speaking, then I certainly don't want to be the one doing it, and I don't even want to be watching.

There was no way that I could have commented fairly upon the film. So, I decided that the best thing to do would be to publicly distance myself from it, in as genial and engaging a way as possible by not heaping scorn upon the filmmakers or the movie industry, but by wishing them well with the work, and by saying that it was a distinct entity from my book.

That way, if the film did well, that was not to the credit of my book. If the film did badly, that was not to the detriment of my book. Basically, they were two completely separate things. And with that established, I would be quite happy to take the money, to not go and see the film, and that would be fine by me.

And that seemed to work. As far as I know, the *From Hell* movie–while it is really nothing like my book, apart from a couple of scenes here and there–was probably at least a decent attempt at trying to film a book that is, when you think about it, pretty much unfilmable. I believe that they did probably as good a job as anybody could, the Hughes Brothers. They and probably did as good a job as anybody could of making a film out of *From Hell*. Which is to say, that they still probably shouldn't have bothered, in that the end result would have so little resemblance to anything that I wrote that they might just as well have made their own Jack the Ripper film, with their own story.

But, that went fairly well. There were no ugly repercussions from it. I still haven't seen the film, nor do I intend to. But, it passed without any unpleasantness.

The League of Extraordinary Gentlemen was the next film that was made of my work. And I took the same position with this film that I would just let Hollywood get on with it. I wouldn't be going to see the finished production. I would be accepting the money that they were giving me for it. But, I would be keeping a distance between the work and the filmed version, the way that I had done with *From Hell*.

Now, this was starting to feel a little bit to feel uneasy for me. Because I was realizing that, while I might have a very clear distinction in my mind as to the differences between the book and the film, the average cinema-goer is not even going to be aware that it was based upon a book. Or, if they are, they're probably going to assume that the film is a pretty fair reflection of what was in the book.

And I was starting to feel uneasy about that. Because it seemed to me that, no matter how much I might like to think that I'd distanced my original work from the film adaptation, I realized that, in the greater part of the public's mind, that was not the case at all. And, what could I say? That was starting to make me feel uncomfortable. Then, we had a problem with a lawsuit.

This was after the film had come out, *The League of Extraordinary Gentlemen*. Apparently, a Hollywood screen writer had brought a lawsuit against the makers of the film, suggesting that they had stolen an idea from a group of Victorian characters that he had proposed to them in a screenplay a few years before.

Now, it wasn't that really any of the characters from my book were included in the list of characters in his film. But, I believe that some of the characters that had been added at the studio's insistence, such as Dorian Gray and possibly Tom Sawyer, that a couple of these characters did seem to have some similarities with the ones in his screenplay.

Now, the person bringing this lawsuit realized that it was a bit of a tricky case, given that the film was based upon my comic–or, at least, supposedly so–and that he couldn't really bring a lawsuit upon the film alone on that basis. There was an argument put forward that apparently the head of 20th Century Fox, or somebody of importance at 20th Century Fox, had stolen the ideas from his screenplay and then had phoned me up–because, apparently, we're such close friends–and had suggested that I should write *The League of Extraordinary Gentlemen* as a smoke screen to conceal his act of creative larceny. To which I agreed, apparently, and so I put together this *The League of Extraordinary Gentlemen* comic purely to cover up theft by somebody at 20th Century Fox.

Now, I have got no axe to grind about the honesty of people in the movie industry. For all I know, the people at 20th Century Fox may have stolen this person's ideas. But what really upset me was the fact that this has been phrased in such a way as to make it sound like I had been a party to this and, moreover, that I got my ideas from Hollywood film writers who, to be frank, are not people that I've got the most literary respect for in the world.

It felt like the film industry, which I wanted nothing to do with, suddenly was dragging my name into a grubby, sleazy little tort case. Now, I understood that the suit wasn't being brought against me. But, my name had been involved.

So, I went down to London, into the depths of Soho, where I was cross-examined by VideoLink for ten hours, where I was talking and answering all of the questions put to me by both Fox's defense attorneys and by the lawyer for the plaintiff. And that was quite wearying.

Also, during the course of this court case, it was revealed to me that one of the producers on the film, for a joke, apparently, had sent prank e-mails to the people bringing the suit saying that, yes, he knew for a fact that I had stolen the idea of *The League of Extraordinary Gentlemen* from this other guy's screenplay, and then he'd signed these e-mails with some bogus nom de plume.

Obviously, I've since cut off all contact with this person. But he seemed to be completely mystified by my response, because "It had just been a joke." I presume it was one of those Hollywood jokes; you can always spot them because they actually aren't funny.

But, whether it was a joke or not, he was communicating with somebody who was bringing a lawsuit based upon the idea that I'd stolen my ideas from a Hollywood screen writer. He was sending them an e-mail saying that, yes, I had–for a joke.

This was apparently what lost the case, as far as I understand it, for 20th Century Fox. Because they were not actually able to adequately explain that joke. And I believe that they settled with the plaintiffs, which is almost as good as saying, "Yes, we admit it. They were all true, your allegations."

So, at that point, I decided that I wanted nothing else to do with the film industry for the rest of my life. The film industry seemed to me to be completely rotten. It's not even a medium that I'm that fond of, to be

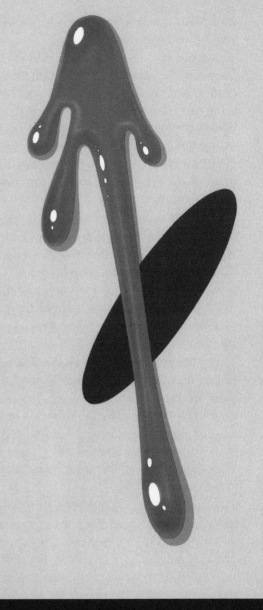

WINNER OF THE
HUGO AWARD

WATCHMEN

ALAN MOORE
DAVE GIBBONS

And then people started to talk about options for *Watchmen* and *V for Vendetta*, which by that point I had realized that I had no say in, because they were owned by DC Comics, both of those titles. So, whether they got made into films or not was a thing that wasn't within my control.

perfectly honest. There are a lot of things that I enjoy a lot more than I enjoy film.

I'd never really been interested in having my work adapted for film. So I decided that the only thing that I could do that would be taking the high ground on the issue would be to refuse any future payments for films that were made of my work. This is for the films such as *Watchmen* and *V for Vendetta*, things that were owned by companies and which I no longer owned, and where I didn't have a say whether they were filmed or not. In the instance where they were filmed, I would not be accepting money for them, and I would be asking for my name in consequence to be taken off of the films.

I also decided that, with the books that I did own, but where I'd co-authored them with an artist, it wouldn't really be fair of me to deny the artist the chance to make the money if that's what they wanted. So I said that, in those cases, the film people could talk to the artist. I would not be accepting any of the money, and I would not want my name upon the film. But if they and the artist wanted to come to some agreement, then that was fine by me. Which I thought was about the fairest arrangement that I could think of.

So then, just a couple of days after making this pronouncement, and while I was probably still wondering a little bit if it had been a bit drastic–even for me–to turn down such large sums of money, I received a phone call from Karen Berger. She sounded very chirpy and happy, and was telling me that it was good news, that I'd be receiving a lot of money before the end of the year as a result of the fact that there was a John Constantine film being made, or "Constanteen," as I am told that we should now refer to him.

And so I said, equally affably, to Karen that, well, it was nice of her to call and let me know that, but I'd got a new position regarding films. So, regarding the money that was going to be paid to me, if they could just pay that to the artists who were involved in the creation of John Constantine–and particularly Rick Veitch, who was the first person to actually draw him in a comic, and yet who wouldn't have been eligible for any money on the character, apparently—I would appreciate it. So I said, "Well, give my share of the money, share it out amongst these various people, John Totleben and a few other people, so that everybody, including Rick Veitch, gets the same amount." This would have been probably $70,000 or something like that, divided up between four or five people.

I said, "Yeah, just divide it up amongst the other artists concerned. Make sure that my name doesn't go on the film, and then everybody will be happy." And I told her that, "This is my policy from now on. I don't want any of the money from the films, and don't want my name on the films."

Karen said that she wasn't sure that they were going to put my name on the film, anyway. And, I said, well, that didn't matter. I wasn't going to accept the money just because they weren't putting my name on the film. I just wanted them to divide the money up amongst the artists and, whether they'd been intending to put my name on the film or not, as long as my name didn't actually end up on the film, then I would be perfectly happy with life.

And that seemed to work fine. Obviously, this was because they had never had any intention of putting my name on the film because, as it turns out, the Constantine movie was made under that same open-ended deal that The Swamp Thing film had been made under. Constantine was a character that appeared in Swamp Thing, so, therefore, the filmmakers had got the right to make a movie of it, and use any of the materials they wanted. But, like I say, for whatever reason, it worked out fine as far as I was concerned.

A little bit after that, I got an option payment. It was only $7,000, something like that, on the *V for Vendetta* movie, which I'd not known was still an ongoing proposition. So, I spoke to Karen and said, "Okay, I'd like this money to be sent to David Lloyd, the same as we did with the Constantine film." And she was saying that, as with the Constantine film, I would have to sign something that said that I was happy to hand my money over to David Lloyd. And, as with the Constantine film, I said that I've got no problem with that, and that Karen should just send me the paperwork and I'd sign it and send it back to her. And then they could send Dave the money. I think that was the only option payment.

Then, the next I knew was that the film had gone into production, and now they're talking about handing me the big production payment. And I got a couple of phone calls telling me that maybe I'd want to reconsider taking my name off this, because actually it was very faithful to my book. And that it was so faithful to my book that I might want to reconsider taking my name off this–and also reconsider sending the money to Dave Lloyd.

And I said, "Well, no. The option payment was sent to Dave Lloyd. I'm not suddenly going to change my mind now. And, anyway, I'm entirely lacking in confidence that this film is going to be anything like my book."

It seemed to me that it would probably have a few set pieces that were taken or lifted from my book, and these would be set into a context that was entirely the filmmaker's and would probably have nothing to do with my book at all. Now, there was a lot of hemming and hawing, but, eventually, I received this piece of paper saying that I would sign my money over to David Lloyd. And I signed that and sent it straight back.

Now, it was around about this point when there was a press release from Warner Bros. in which one of the producers, Joe Silver, of the *V for Vendetta* movie, had apparently issued a statement... No. No, now let me backtrack a little bit here. Let me backtrack.

I had received, a few weeks before this, a phone call out of the blue–I have no idea where he got my number from--out of the blue from one of the Wachowski brothers. I was in the middle of work, but I tried to be as polite as possible. He was asking if he couldn't meet with me to talk about this film. And I was explaining to him that, no, I wasn't accepting any of the money for it, I didn't want any connection with it, but I wished him well with it. That I wished him good luck with it, but that I was engrossed in other work at the moment and I wouldn't be able to meet with him to talk about this film, and really couldn't spare the time to talk about anything for at least for a couple of years, because I'm very busy. I explained that that was no offense to him, and that I wished him well with the film, but I had asked to be left out of it. And at that point he sounded a bit disconsolate and rang off.

And then, later, after I had signed the thing and sent it back to say that the money could go to Dave Lloyd, Joel Silver made his press conference speech in which he said that the Wachowski Brothers had been in touch with Alan Moore; that I was very, very excited about the film; that I was going to be meeting with them real soon so that I could have input, and so we could all sit around and discuss how excited we were about this film, and more in this sort of vein.

Which, I was infuriated by, because it was a flat, knowing lie. Not only that, but this came in the wake of a couple of interviews that I'd done where I'd explained exactly why I no longer wished to have anything to do with film versions of my work, why I was no longer accepting the money, and all the rest of the stuff that I've just described to you.

Now, to have a press release come out from Warner Bros. that makes it sound as if I was being insincere, or lying, when I said those things, that is deeply angering. Especially in the wake of all that I've been through on that wretched League of Extraordinary Gentlemen film, where it was starting to strike me that I was dealing with people who had absolutely no sense of honor whatsoever, who had long since forgotten what the word meant, and who had no qualms about casually implying that everybody else was as dishonorable as they were.

So I thought that, at the very least, this constituted a reminder that it was DC Comics who were publishing *The League of Extraordinary Gentlemen*. So, I phoned up WildStorm and I said to them that, unless this could be sorted out, then I would not be doing any future volumes of *The League of Extraordinary Gentlemen* for WildStorm, and that I would be having nothing to do in the future with DC or any of its subsidiary companies. That I would have, indeed, clauses written into my contracts that said that, even if the small company that I was working for got bought out by DC, that that would void my contract with them.

I said, "Now, this is what will happen if this doesn't get sorted out. But, luckily it is relatively easy to sort this out. All I require, to make this go away, is that–in a forum comparable with that in which the initial press release was issued–if I could just have a modest apology, retraction and clarification." This didn't need to be a humiliating climb-down, and I was not asking anybody to say, "I am a fat liar," even though in reality that was, indeed, the case. I wasn't asking anybody to humiliate themselves like that.

I suggested that if they just said that, "Owing to a misunderstanding, we have reported that Alan Moore blah, blah, blah. Whereas, in fact, Alan Moore blah, blah, blah. We apologize to Mr. Moore for any inconvenience caused."

Now, that wouldn't have been humiliating or injurious, I don't think. And that would have sorted everything out. I pointed out to them that, if they didn't make those corrections and retractions and apologies, I would be severing all contact with DC. That if they refused to make this apology, I would be disowning the works that I had done for DC Comics, and I would be refusing payment for that, as well.

You know, if they had done that, then I would have been happy to continue doing with *The League of Extraordinary Gentlemen* with DC. It could have all continued smoothly. But I said, "In the light of this, can you please get this small retraction? If you can't, then I shall never be working for DC again and, further to that, if my name still goes on this film, despite everything that I have asked for, then I shall be taking my name off of all of the works. I am determined not to be associated with this film. And so, if that means that I take my name off the works as well, then, so be it."

As I explained to Scott Dunbier, although that would cause me a great deal of hardship, and a great deal of wrenching pain to actually disown works that I was very proud of, that I would do it in a split second. And I think that Scott knows me well enough to understand that that was, indeed, the case. He told me that it was taking a while to get this kind of apology.

In fact, it went on for five or six weeks, where I was holding my fire, because DC was saying, "Well, it takes so long dealing with Hollywood people." Eventually, at the end of this five or six weeks, they got back to me via Scott Dunbier, explaining that they could offer me the retraction and clarifying statement in a corner of the DC web site—which is not, forgive me, the same as what I'd asked for; which was to have this clarification issued in a forum as big as that in which the initial press statement had been made.

So I said, "Okay, well that's it for me and DC Comics, then. And, I still want my name taken off of this film." And I reiterated that if my name wasn't taken off of the film, then I would be asking for it to be taken off the books, as well.

At this point, they sounded a bit worried and were saying that they've got this big commemorative *Watchmen* edition coming out. And there was a new [hardcover edition of the] *V for Vendetta* book coming out. This was at a point when I'd spoken to Scott and I said to him, "They are going to be taking my name off of this film, aren't they Scott?" And he said, "Oh, I don't know. The last thing I heard, they were thinking that they were just going to leave it on there."

The future pauses, waits its cue
to happen. He can't see the
streetlamps. He can't see the
skyline for the glow that's
in his eyes.

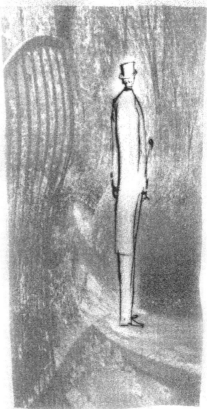

Yeah. Eddie, he started out just doing comics because he loved them, and he wanted to do them in exactly the way that he wanted to do them, which meant that he'd publish them himself in these inexpensive mini-comics. And the work was good enough.

And I said, "Well, in that case, as far as these books of mine that are coming out, if they're going to be coming out with DC knowing that I am going to have my name put on this film, with DC expecting my name to go on this film, whether I like it or not, then DC should also be expecting to be bringing out these books without my name on them." And that kind of seemed to cause a degree of panic.

Now, I certainly don't want to penalize Dave Gibbons, say, and never have done. Dave Gibbons has always stood by me completely in the past where I've had more differences of opinion with DC. He doesn't feel the same way about them that I do, and I respect that. And he respects the way that I feel.

So, I came up with what I thought was a compromise. The compromise was that, "Okay, if you can just get me a little piece of paper–you didn't get me the apology or the retraction or the clarification—but, if you can just get me a little piece of paper signed by someone in authority that says that my name will not be going on this film, then you can go ahead and bring out all the books you want–just as long as I've got that assurance." I mean, how difficult can that be, two or three lines on a piece of paper?

"Get that to me and, most importantly, make sure that I don't get sent any books with my name on them before I have got that piece of paper." I said, "These are not complicated instructions, and I've been messed about quite enough already. Just get this right. Just get me this little piece of paper that assures me that my name will not be going upon this wretched film." Because, by then I had actually had access to a screenplay of the film, and had found out that it was every bit as bad as I'd feared, if not worse.

So, I stressed that they should make sure that I get this piece of paper. And, whatever else happens, make sure that I don't get any books with my name on them in big letters that have been put out by DC Comics before I get this piece of paper.

So, predictably, nothing happened for a number of weeks. I hadn't got my piece of paper. I was told that they were working on it. And then one day I have the Federal Express man come to the door bringing me, not as it turned out, a FedEx copy of my required piece of paper, but a big box containing the new hardback DC edition of *V for Vendetta*. Which, apart from the fact that I had specifically asked for it not to be sent to me, I found had the back cover copy re-jigged to make use of the "Remember,

remember the 5th of November" phrase that was prominent in the film, but was of very little importance in the books.

I didn't take the cling film off of any of these copies that I'd been sent. But, even from a cursory look at the cover, [it was apparent] there had been nobody looking at this in an editorial capacity at any stage during its production. I can only assume that was the case, because if any editorial person had looked at it, then they weren't doing their job.

I mean, there were words entirely missed out of the copy that made absolutely nonsense of it. The phrase "Have a pleasant evening" had been rendered on the back of the book in large display type as "Have a pleasant," and that's it. "Have a pleasant." So, unless the phrase, "Have a pleasant," is something that is current with the teenagers of today that I've just missed out on, it looked to me like it was an obvious mistake that somebody, at some point, surely should have caught if they had had any respect for the work at all.

This was very small potatoes, besides the fact that they'd sent it to me. So, at this point, this was turning out to be one of the longest years of my life. Waiting for these people to send me retractions, apologies, a simple signed letter stating their intent. All of these small things that would have cost them nothing, and which had been making my life for much of the last year a complete misery. All with occasional little high points, like the delivery of these *V for Vendetta* books, which went straight out and into a skip, in dumpster, in the backyard, which we've got for some building work.

That following morning–and very, very early in the morning, it was about 2:00 or 3:00 in the morning–I woke up and I was filled with black, churning rage. I came downstairs, and I phoned up WildStorm. I left a message saying what happened and that I wished for my name to be taken off of the *V for Vendetta* book, and that if they could not do this satisfactorily, I wanted it taken off of everything else that had been published by DC which I did not own—which, pathetically, enough is *The League of Extraordinary Gentlemen*. Out of all of the works that I've done for DC, for WildStorm, for ABC, the only one that I own, or co-own with Kevin, is *The League of Extraordinary Gentlemen*.

And so I said that, "If you can't take my name off of the book, then I want it taken off of all of them." Things trailed on for another couple of months. And then, as the film was about ready to come out, I got a phone call from Karen Berger who said to me that she had been down to talk to Paul Levitz but, no, the Hollywood people were definitely going to put my name on this film and there was nothing that anybody could do about it.

To which I said, "Fair enough, Karen. In that case, I want my name taken off of all of the books, including the ABC books. Everything." And, she said, "Well, we're not going to take your name off them." They weren't going to take my name off of the *V for Vendetta* book.

And I said, "Okay. Well, if you wish to leave it on there, leave it on. But know that the book is unauthorized in the sense of the fact that its author wishes to have no more to do with it. Also, after the current books have sold out, the ones that have been printed prior to this hardback atrocity, you can stop sending me any money for all of these books." She then said that they probably wouldn't stop sending me the money either. So I said that at that point I should decide an arbitrary date, say, mid summer or late summer of 2006, at which point I should stop accepting any of the payments.

Admittedly, since then, having had time to shake off the homicidal rage and come to my senses, I have--perhaps predictably--changed my mind about this. My name was taken off the film, which was all I had ever originally wanted, and it was only the seemingly deliberate actions of DC Comics in telling me that my name wouldn't be removed that had provoked me to this extremity. So, yes, I'll be accepting royalties on my work but, since I don't own it I have no further interest in it, nor do I wish for any future communications with anyone representing DC Comics.

So anyway, I explained to Karen why I was taking this position, and she was saying, "Well, why are you blaming DC for something that Hollywood's doing?" which is something that Scott had said, as well. And I said that the only reason this was happening was because DC Comics had stolen *Watchmen* and *V for Vendetta* from me in the first place, way back in the 80s.

So for DC to then turn around and say that they were blameless, when they had taken this work from me, they had pimped it out to their Hollywood associates and parent company, and were then saying, "This is not our fault," was disingenuous. And I said that I'd given them plenty of opportunities, and that I'd always gladly signed my money away to the artists since then on the understanding that this was a reciprocal deal. That that was the nature of deals, that they were reciprocal. And that I was signing my money away on the understanding that my name was not going to be going on these films.

At this point, Karen said, "Well, I don't remember you not wanting to have your name on the film as part of the deal." And I said, "Karen, it wasn't part of the deal. It was the whole deal," as Karen, surely knew. And it struck me that this was probably a good industry to be getting out of, and I felt very badly used.

The next day, I had Scott Dunbier call me up to tell me excitedly that I was going to be sent a piece of paper which I could sign saying that I didn't want my name to go on this film. And I said, "Well, why did Karen phone me yesterday and tell me that that wasn't going to happen?" And Scott said that he didn't know anything about that; that, as far as he knew, I was getting this piece of paper that, if I just signed it and sent it back, would say that my name wasn't going to go on this film. It was like I've got to give them permission to not put my name on this film—which, if they'd have asked me for at any point in the past, I would have gladly done.

And so I said "Fine. All right, at least that is a result in that my name will not be going on this film. Unfortunately, it comes far too late. If this could have come two weeks ago, or six weeks ago, or just before DC sent me those books, then everything would have been fine and there'd have been no need for all this ridiculous stuff. But, I'm afraid, yes, I'll sign this thing. I'll send it back to them, and hopefully my name will not go on this film. But, it doesn't change anything. I really want out of the entire comics business, or at least the major industrial part of it."

So we, me and Kevin, decided that The League would henceforth be published by an evil multinational conglomerate formed of Top Shelf Comics over in the States, and Knockabout Comics over here, which are small and honorable companies. And I really do want those to be practically the only companies that I'm dealing with in terms of comics in the future.

And my actual work in comics in the future will probably be very limited. It will be limited to the stuff that I am passionate about and the stuff that I own, which will include *The League of Extraordinary Gentlemen*, the forthcoming *Lost Girls*, and any other pieces that I come out with. So I'll probably still be doing a certain amount of work in comics, but it will no longer be by any means the majority of the work I do, and we'll be doing those comics with them.

I felt very, very good once I'd done all that, and burned those bridges. I felt a great weight lift off of me. Yeah, there's a certain amount of financial insecurity, and all of that normal human stuff. But, the actual relief to know that I will not be working for those people again was more than worth it. I have been trying to get away from DC Comics since the 1980s, when I first realized what they were.

Back then, I had gone into my relationship with them in good faith, and I think that they had done quite well out of it. And when they suggested that I might want to create something that could be creator-owned under this wonderful new contract that they'd got, which would mean that as soon as the book went out of print it would return to the ownership of the creators, then I was very glad to enter into that. And, in fact, it was me who suggested to Dave Lloyd that, since this was such a good deal, we might as well let DC publish *V for Vendetta*, as well as *Watchmen*.

And it soon became apparent that, back then, there had never been a comic book that had had a shelf life of longer than a couple of months. There had never been a comic album that had a shelf life of more than a year. Nothing had happened like *Watchmen* before.

BB: Right. But just to be clear, we're talking about the English speaking market, here, right?

AM: In the English speaking market, yeah. Yeah, of course, there have been a lot of things in the French market and stuff. But for the English speaking market, and for the American market, there hadn't really been any precedents for *Watchmen*. I think that we soon started to realize that that meant that this would probably be kept in print forever, and that therefore we'd never have the work returned to us. At this point, I started...

Well, I became very, very cross with DC Comics, who had represented themselves to me as my friends, as people who really, really appreciated the fact that I was working for their company and achieving such marvelous results, and that–to a certain degree–I was reshaping the market in a way that was very favorable to DC, and to comics in general. And then we were told that no, there wouldn't be any redrafting of the contract, and that, yeah, they did own this stuff forever. As long as DC kept it in print, it was theirs, and they were never going to let it go out of print.

At that point, I did the only honorable thing that I could do and said, "In that case, I shall complete the work that I am doing for you, and I shan't be working for DC again." There were other things in the mix. There were some other indignities. There was a certain stinginess on DC's part to hand over the full royalties on the *Watchmen* merchandise. And then there was the labeling of comic books as being for mature readers or whatever, which I also disagreed with. But this was all in the mix, and it was largely the fact that I felt that I'd been treated badly by the company that made me say that I would not be working for them again, which was something that I was quite happy doing.

And that's how things stood up until I was working, I think, for Awesome Comics, or whatever Rob Liefeld's pet project was called at that time, when I received a phone call saying that the company had gone bust and that there would be no more Awesome Comics. Now, that would mean that the various artists who I enjoyed working with, and who I had been able to find work for, they would be out of work. It wasn't so much of a problem for me, because I don't really have a great deal of problem finding work in the comic industry. But, the people that I was working with, I felt it would be letting them down, perhaps quite seriously.

We then got a phone call from Awesome, saying that DC had approached them, saying that they would like to rescue the company by buying it out–on the condition that Alan Moore was part of the deal.

Now, I didn't actually have any contract with Awesome at that point. And so I said, "No, I never want to work for DC again." I was a bit startled that they should have tried to buy an entire company just to secure the services of one individual. And I would have thought that that must have seemed a little desperate.

You would have thought that DC Comics, at some point during its sixty-year history, would have come up with a few comparable talents that meant that it could let me go. You would have thought. But, anyway, I sort of rebuffed them and said that, "No, I'm not particularly concerned about whether Awesome Comics collapses or not, and I'm certainly not going to promise to work for DC in an effort to save it."

So, instead, I went off with the artists that I was in contact with and looked for somewhere else. I'd already been talking to Jim Lee about the possibility of a genuinely creator-owned book, *The League of Extraordinary Gentlemen*. Now, when I decided that I could do with a raft of mainstream comic titles that I could write and that various friends of mine and associates could work on, Jim seemed a decent person to approach–because he is a very decent person. So I came up with the proposals for the ABC line because I figured that since, in terms of mainstream comics, it wasn't a creator-owned deal, there would be more money up front in compensation. And I decided that, all right, because I trusted Jim Lee, and understood that he would give me a fair deal, I was quite happy to do the books, except for *The League of Extraordinary Gentlemen*, under those work-for-hire terms.

So, the contracts were signed, the various artists were contacted, and some of the first scripts had been written. And, basically, the artists had all been told that they were going to have regular work for a considerable period. At that point, I was coming back from a holiday in Wales, when Jim Lee and Scott Dunbier flew over here to break the news to me that DC Comics had bought WildStorm–which put me in a bit of a position.

I really did not want to work for DC Comics again. And it was pretty transparent that that must have been at least part of the reason behind them buying WildStorm, given what they'd already attempted with Awesome. On the other hand, to have refused to work for them would have meant breaking the contract and, most importantly, breaking my word to the artists.

After thinking about it for a while, it seemed to me that, if it was a choice between going back on my word to myself and going back on my word to the artists, then the best thing–the thing that I could live with–was going back on my word to myself. So, uneasily, I entered into the ABC deal, determined to give it my best shot and to do the absolute best comics that I possibly could.

I was initially promised that there wouldn't be any interference from DC, but this didn't turn out to be the case.

In fact, from quite early on it did seem that there was almost some sort of deliberate malice, or something like that, that was being directed at my books in particular. Trivial, tiny things that may never have been done to other people's books, like the Marvel vaginal douche ad in *The League of*

"I don't have any strong nostalgic associations with comics. I'm not going to rule out that there might be the odd sort of nostalgic maggot riding around somewhere deep in my heart, but, by and large, I don't have a nostalgic attachment with comics anymore."

Extraordinary Gentlemen, which lead to an entire issue's run being pulped rather than be distributed, and their decision to not allow publication of the Cobweb story that had all of these apparently sensational revelations about L. Ron Hubbard and Jack Parsons that already, for the most part, had already been published by DC in a another book. All of these things that happened, they seemed a little personal to me, although I tried not to take them personally. [Laughs] I was also hearing...

There was a friend of a friend who apparently worked in the Warner Bros. boardroom, who had said that right from the outset of the ABC deal, apparently DC's Publisher, Paul Levitz, had felt that this was some sort of contest between me and him. That I was "fucking with him," and that he was going to show me what for.

Now, this is somebody that I never even think about.

BB: Have you ever had a run-in, or perhaps some kind of disagreement with him, prior to all of this?

AM: Well, no. But he has behaved quite oddly to me ever since my first meeting with him, the first time I went over there. I remember his first words to me after I'd just arrived in New York were, "So, Alan Moore. You are my greatest mistake." [Laughs] Sort of ambiguous, to say the least. I just figured it was a kind of a neurotic, American business thing that I didn't quite understand. And there was...

I'm not sure whether it might be to do with the fact that, before he was a publisher, he was a comic writer. I don't know whether that's got anything to do with it. I did sometimes detect, in my early days of working for the American market, that there were a number of comic writers who perhaps previously had enjoyed quite a reputation for their writing, who suddenly seemed to feel threatened, or displaced, or overlooked, or something.

I wasn't in a competition with anybody. I was just trying to do the best stuff that I could. But, I did hear certain reported comments, and things like that, that suggested that there was a certain amount of mistrust and fear amongst certain elements of the creative community over there. Whether this extended to the current Publisher of DC or not, I don't know. But, that's the only thing that I could think of.

I mean, it's not like I ever met the guy more than a couple of times. It's the only thing I could think of that might provide some sort of motivation for the somewhat remarkable way in which I've been treated by the company. Given that there probably aren't that many other single creators who have done that company as much good, as far as I know, I know of no other single creator who has been left quite as embittered as I am with the way that they've been treated.

I mean, after the problems surrounding *Watchmen* and *V for Vendetta* that caused me to depart from DC the first time, there was a sudden change in emphasis upon their contracts. I believe that Neil Gaiman owns Mr. Punch, along with Dave McKean. A lot of the authors who followed me had the benefit of much more favorable contracts. And I believe that Neil had even suggested to them that they could sort out of all of this horrible mess with me by simply re-drafting the contract to *Watchmen* and *V for Vendetta* to the later model, which everybody was now enjoying.

They declined.

I suppose at this point I ought to no longer even be bothered with what it might be, or what might be behind it. I no longer care. It's some sort of strange, thwarted behavior by people in an industry which I entered with good intentions, and which, I think, I can justifiably say has been enough to try the patience of a saint. My love of the comics medium is what has kept me going in this misbegotten industry for so long.

But, there are other things that I love just as much, if not more, than comics. So the timing of this whole event has been a bit unfortunate, I guess. I mean, at least in terms of my continuing relation with the comic business. But I don't feel that it's been unfortunate for me. I feel very liberated by it.

And, given that it seems that DC were willing to buy entire companies in order to secure my services, which is...

That's the behavior of a rich stalker, you know? It's sort of... [General laughter]

BB: Sorry to laugh, but, yes, it is.

AM: It is. I mean, if it was a person doing it rather than a corporation, then it would look very, very odd indeed. And to me it looks just as odd, if not odder. But it's a big, and supposedly important, corporation. And it also seems that, if they are prepared to go to those lengths to secure more services, then really I have to do something drastic in order to put myself beyond their reach. I would sooner starve than work for those people again. I never want anything to do with them.

And that goes for most comic book publishers, not just for DC. But DC are emblematic of a wider malaise in the comics industry. And, no, I'm not saying that I'd have been treated any better by Marvel Comics.

There's something about publishing, big publishing in America, and probably, all over the world, that–in terms of comics–it's not what I wanted for comics. And it certainly isn't being done with the people who are actually doing the work in mind. There's something really shameful about the comics field, with its continuing refusal to grow up and become a proper, grown up medium, a respectable medium, for the 21st century. As long as it can hold on to its grubby little practices, it will do. And let us not forget that those practices have been very, very grubby at times. And that the only times when any of these companies have made any concessions has been when they've absolutely had to, as when DC was shamed into giving a pittance to Jerry Siegel and Joe Schuster, when they were desperate that their names should be on the first Superman film.

I've thought about that, that actually my position, in that I want my name taken off, I'm kind of like the bizarro Jerry Siegel in many respects. [Laughs] The irony is not lost on me.

BB: They can't seem to figure you out. I think they're completely mystified by you–but especially by your directness, and honesty.

AM: I'm what I seem to be. This was another reason why I was so depressed during a lot of last year. It was because, not only were they showing no signs of actually doing anything about the problems that I brought up, they also all seemed completely bewildered by my moral position. I didn't seem to be able to...

Even people who were sympathetic seemed absolutely bewildered by moral points that, from my background, would seem kind of obvious, you know? It was...

Like I say, it kind of made me rethink a lot of my relationships within the comics industry over the years. And it seems to me that, at the end of the day, probably the comics industry has done better out of our association than I, myself, have out of our association. I think that the comics industry has made more of its association with me than I have really done with my association with it. And that's because the only thing that the comic industry has ever been able to offer me are things that I don't particularly want.

I don't want unreasonably huge amounts of money. I don't want fame. I don't want any of the things that are really on offer. What I want is a position of self-respect in which I own the work which I produce. And they do not seem able to offer me that, for the most part.

So, after 20, 25 years of banging my head upon the same brick wall, just as a lot of other creators before me have damaged their brains in the same endeavor, I think it's about time to call it quits. Like I say, the comic field has perhaps not turned out as I had best hoped it would.

I felt, back in the 80s, that I was in part responsible for providing a tremendously invigorating jolt to comic books. I wasn't the only one, but I was one of a few people who quite radicalized the field in the 1980s, and have changed things round to what has probably been almost everybody's benefit.

I don't know. I feel that if the comic industry actually wants to be a grown up industry that produces grown up work by grown up creators, then it had better grow up. It's already too late as far as I'm concerned. But if it wants to have any creators of any stature in the future, then why should they bother to work in comics where they'll almost certainly be robbed, and where they will be dealing with people who don't appear to have a shred of honor between them?

Like I said, I think that I brought quite a bit to comics, and I am nevertheless very, very happy to be, for all intents and purposes, withdrawing from them at the moment. I've had an awful lot of fun. I've worked with some wonderful people. And, at the end of the day, there are about five books that I actually own, out of the dozens of books that I've actually written. And that can't be right.

So, the cleanest sort of severance that I could think of was to pursue the actions that I have done. That seemed to be the best way of removing myself from a situation which I have long since ceased to feel comfortable about.

BB: Are there any other lessons you've learned, aside from "Make sure you own your work"?

AM: Yeah, there's one really, really important lesson that I've learned from this, and that is: "Don't trust Whitey." [General laughter] That's about it. I can't think of anything much more edifying than that.

Of course, I've learned tons about my craft, and I'm very grateful for that. And I've produced some great work. But, by and large, I think that I may be incompatible with mainstream American business processes. That is perhaps the fairest and least hurtful way of putting it. Because there were an awful lot of people over there, even sympathetic people, that did not seem to understand why I was so upset, why I was doing the things that I was doing.

I didn't expect them to agree with me, but I at least expected some degree of basic human understanding. These moral points, which would seem fairly self-evident to me, were being looked at with open-mouthed, slack-jawed mystification.

And it seems to me, at least as far as the business culture is concerned, that there's something a bit wrong with the way that the American mindset appears to be going at the moment. This is only said from my perspective. I'm not even claiming that it's from an English perspective. This is, perhaps, just purely me.

Part of the relief that I felt about divorcing myself from DC Comics is that I no longer feel comfortable about working for big American businesses, or big businesses of any sort. But, at this particular moment, I have a special aversion towards big American businesses, because their business policy does seem to be remarkably similar to American foreign policy of the moment, but writ small.

There is a sense of, "The situation is whatever we say it is." Doesn't matter what the facts might be, "Whatever situation we can insist upon,

DC UNIVERSE: THE STORIES OF ALAN MOORE

Part of the relief that I felt about divorcing myself from DC Comics is that I no longer feel comfortable about working for big American businesses, or big businesses of any sort.

that is reality." Doesn't matter whether it's fair, doesn't matter whether it's true. "If we just insist upon our view of reality, then everybody else will have to go along with it." And [their current opinion holds] that, basically, everybody other than America itself is a resource, and it's something there to be used.

In terms of how the comics industry treats its artists and writers, and I'm sure this is not going to be a great surprise to everybody, but it treats them as a resource. It treats them as fuel rods. It has got no respect for them as individuals. It will work them to death in the hope of getting out a few more books from them. And then, when they're dead, it can publish fulsome obituaries and release all of their work in commemorative editions--and continue to make money out of them. It's like they're replaceable.

Like Jack Kirby, one of the finest artists ever to grace this medium. By the end of the day him, along with a lot of comic artists who, perhaps, who had gone a little past their peak, have practically been pilloried and lampooned as "past it." And, since they're no longer selling the books that they used to, they were discarded with but a, "So, who needs them?" That is shameful.

The only people who have made this medium–the only people who have ever formed this medium–are the people who write it, who draw it, and who letter it and who color it. There have occasionally been one or two editors that are better than others, yeah, certainly. Yeah, there have been some good editors in this medium. The majority of them, however, don't really do an awful lot of editing. They seem to be mainly concerned with...

They're kind of production managers, in charge of scheduling. That's not editing.

It's the artist and writers who are responsible for every comic book which you've ever enjoyed. And, in most cases, it's the artists and writers who have died distressed and penniless, or alcoholics, or suicidal; whereas, the people at the companies have tended to do rather well, and to have suffered a lot less stress in their dealings with the business.

It isn't right. And I can't really look at comics these days without seeing this immense line of cheated ghosts standing behind every colorful superhero character. And especially when I consider what the comics publishers have made out of the film industry.

One of the things that I learned was that, in fact, the comics that they produce are no longer important, even to the people who are in charge of their production. I genuinely do not believe that the people at the big companies are concerned about comics at all.

I think an indicator of this is that they were prepared for me to sever all of my contact with them, rather than to risk offending a movie producer who had lied about me. It seems to me–and this has, for a long time been, the opinion in the comics industry itself–that DC, for an awful long while, have been terrified that Warner Bros. are just going to turn the DC offices into a car lot or something; that they are aware of their fairly lowly position in the pecking order of things, and that the only reason why Warner Bros. keeps DC around is because, once in a while, one of the characters that they have stolen, like Wonder Woman, or Superman, or Batman, can be turned into a very healthy movie franchise, a television series, a line of toys, or whatever.

So that really means that, increasingly, this is what the comics medium is becoming. Certainly that's the case in America. It's becoming a kind of pumpkin patch to grow movie franchises. And I've been looking at a lot of those Marvel movie franchises, movie franchises where there will be no creator's name attached, other than probably Stan Lee.

I don't remember a huge furor for a Steve Ditko revival around the time of Spiderman's movie's release, for example.

BB: Right.

AM: In fact, Steve Ditko's another one of those people who's been completely abandoned by the comics industry. Here's somebody who, along with Jack Kirby, was probably responsible for shaping a lot of the way that we see contemporary comics. But, "He kind of stiffened up. His later drawing wasn't quite as good as that early drawing, was it? So we don't really need him anymore do, we? And we're under no obligation to him! We're under no obligation to treat him with dignity in his old age." It's...

I don't want to be a part of a medium like that–or, rather, I don't want to be a part of a business like that. The comics medium, in its pure form, such as it still is, is a thing I shall always love.

And I should stress that there are still some wonderful people who are working in comics. But I would say that you're more likely to find them on the margins. I don't think you're likely to find them in the main tent anymore where the big name acts are performing. I think you're more likely to find it in the ragged margins of the industry, where you've got people who seem to have an honest voice, who seem to be saying what they mean and to be unafraid to say it.

Yeah, there are still some very notable creators within the field, but they are mainly on the margins. I have been, I think, disappointed with some of the center ring acts seen in comics lately. But this is probably just a reflection of my tastes having changed, rather than any fault of the people concerned.

If I read comics these days it's by people like the wonderful Peter Kuper, you know? There is somebody who is elegant as hell and completely fearless in his choice of material. Joe Sacco is someone who is kind, committed and humane—and, above everything, is not currently engaged in beautiful, but ultimately empty, stylistic exercises.

Which is something that I do find an awful lot throughout the mainstream of comics, and even through some of the more exalted areas of the medium, the sort of the more high brow areas. I find that the style of the execution is marvelous but–as with an awful lot of phenomena in the 21st century–there seems to be an awful lot of attention to the surface, whereas, the actual depth of content quite often seem to be very lacking.

BB: And that's something that both Sacco and Kuper really do excel at.

AM: Absolutely. And it's because of their content that their work succeeds.

And there are plenty of others. They are both in the field of sociological documentary, or political satire. That does seem to be one of the areas that comics is scoring highly in.

There are people like Marjane Satrapi, who produced Persepolis, the book about growing up in Iran. Yeah, that was a fantastic piece of work.

She's a very clear, new voice.

What can I say? Those are mostly documentary and political cartoonists, but they are very, very welcome and necessary at the moment.

In terms of fiction, there are perhaps less really outstanding things happening in comics at the moment. This is not to deplore the talents of any of the people who are doing good work--and there are some people who are doing very good work--but, again, I tend to think it's more on the margins.

People like Carla Speed McNeil [Finder]. She is very, very good. She's got an incredibly proficient drawing style, and her story telling abilities are every bit as good. And there are a number of people who I'm sure I shall remember as soon as I put the phone down on this interview that I should have mentioned. I certainly don't mean to say that there's nothing good going on in comics.

But, on the center stage, there's very little that interests me. I can see its merits, but they're not merits that I place a great deal of stock in. Like I said, that is just purely a matter of taste.

However, I would probably have to say--and this might be just my own extremism talking, or my alarmism--but I think that probably the greatest enemy of the comics medium at the moment is the comics industry. I think that if the comics industry is allowed to continue in its normal rapacious fashion, then there's going to be very, very little left of the comics medium. Yes, there is respect for the good comic books that have been done, but most people...

You can tell from the movie reviews what the common view of the comics medium is. Even the ones that are not of comic related titles, if the movie reviewer absolutely wants to insult some film, he will suggest that it's got a comic book plot, or comic book characters, with "comic book" being used as a simile for illiterate.

And then there was a comment upon the Sin City adaptation, which I've not seen, but I know that there was a thing in the Times over here, which said that it was "a misogynistic piece of work--but then, all comics are misogynistic."

And I know that my daughter, Leah, and a number of other women comic creators sent an e-mailed correction to the Times pointing out that, actually, not all comics are misogynistic, and it's a bit of a lazy accusation to be made on the basis of one film–or one comic for that matter.

I don't think that movies are doing comics any favor at all, other than making a great deal of money for a selected range of lucky creators, amongst which I no longer count myself.

BB: And, of course, the stockholders...

AM: Of the companies. Absolutely! But, I don't think it's doing my beloved medium any good.

BB: Right.

AM: Comics pundits seem to get very excited when there's a rash of new comic-related movies coming out. They always seem to be convinced that this is going to be the big breakthrough, this is what is going to bring all of those customers flooding into the shops.

Some filmgoers, they've seen the *From Hell* movie, say. So then they're going to come rushing into the shops to buy this 600-page book in which Johnny Depp does not appear at all, and in which the character that he played is now a sort of a 50ish chubby sort of British Police Commodore from Dorset; where it's in black and white; and where it's got pages upon pages of appendices that make it almost something that they'd have to read for a school essay, or for a test, rather than for the sort of fairly lightweight enjoyment that they go to the movies for?

It's not going to happen, frankly. You might get these occasional blips of an increased sale of such and such a comic after a movie has come out. But I don't think it does the comics medium any good in the long run, because most of these films are no where near as good as the actual comics that they were made of. And yet that is the impression that most of the film viewers are taking away with them.

BB: Right. When the film doesn't work, the comic gets blamed, rather than the adaptation, or even the filmmakers.

SOPHISTICATED SUSPENSE

75¢
37
JUNE 85

SWAMP THING

BY ALAN MOORE, RICK VEITCH & JOHN TOTLEBEN

That was why the second Swamp Thing film featured ideas and lines of butchered dialogue that had been taken from my comparatively thoughtful comics, making them travesties of my work, basically, which I wasn't too happy about.

AM: Of course. Yeah. And, because I have been so voluble about separating myself from the films, most of the reviews of films made of my books have actually mentioned the fact that I've distanced myself from them, if not refused to have anything to do with them altogether. And most of them say, well, this is not as good as the comic book was, which is gratifying. But there are still an awful lot of lazy reviewers out there. I've read reviews of *The League of Extraordinary Gentlemen* film that make it sound like I was the person who came up with the ridiculous idea of putting Tom Sawyer and Dorian Gray in it, and as if the film was an accurate representation of anything that was in my book.

So that was one of the things which was making me uneasy, even before all of this business started, along with the fact that I don't really necessarily trust the public. I don't trust them to bother to distinguish between a film and the source that it was adapted from.

BB: Well, this brings up a topic that I know you want to talk about, and one I'm really interested in, myself. And that is the idea that this is not what you would have wanted comics to be, ideally.

AM: Yeah.

BB: So, what is your ideal vision of the medium, then?

AM: Well, you have to remember that when I got into comics I was seven. But at that point, I was just purely interested in the fabulous and fascinating characters. When I really got into comics as an art form I was around about 14, and I was attending one of the first British comic conventions in this country. I was an associate member of the first two, which meant that I didn't attend, but I went to the third one, which I think was in 1969.

British fandom back then was very, very different to American fandom. For one thing, the first American Fanzines, which had been started by people like the excellent Roy Thomas and Jerry Bails, for example, they were already nostalgic. They were looking back upon a Golden Age of comics, the comics of the 1940s, and there was already a sense of pervasive nostalgia in American fandom, which, I believe, started out in the late 50s with EC Comics fandom. It then grew in the early 60s, with a few mainstream comic fanzines, including the original Alter Ego, and things like that.

Now, British fandom didn't really start until 1967, or maybe 1966, which was only a difference of a few years. But, back then, there was a big difference between 1963 and 1967. At least there was over here [in England]. So, it was around about 1966 that things really started to catch fire in terms of the spirit of the times.

So, basically what I'm saying is that most of those early English comic fans were hippies, or at least proto-hippies or would-be hippies. They were all hanging out at the only comic and science fiction shop in Britain, which was called Dark They Were and Golden-Eyed, named from a Ray Bradbury short story's title, and which serves to give you the flavor of the times. That shop was run by a marvelous archetypal English hippie called Bram Stokes. His name was Derek Stokes, but everybody called him Bram, because of Bram Stoker. And Steve Moore, himself being a budding hippie, was one of the people who organized the first two or three conventions.

And there was an atmosphere. There were only about 100 people there. It was marvelous, it was great. It's something unimaginable today. There were 100 people there and, because there's no point in trying to advertise your goods to 100 people, none of the comic companies were the slightest bit interested. So there was nobody representing any of the companies there. There were a number of artists who were often older men who were astonished and delighted to find that there was anybody who cared about their work at all. And amongst the fans there was, to a large degree, a unity of purpose that all of us ascribed to, perhaps because of the spirit of the times. All of us wanted to see the comics medium progress. We were all listening to progressive music on John Peel's radio shows. The 60s seemed to be a very progressive time, and we wanted to see the art form that we were interested in progressing.

So we applauded people like Jim Steranko, Neal Adams; people who were actually pushing the medium forward, trying to make it do things that it hadn't done before. We went berserk when we discovered Eisner through the Harvey Spirit reprints that were done in the mid-60s. And EC Comics. But, it wasn't a nostalgia for Eisner or for EC Comics–these were things that we were discovering for the first time. We hadn't got time to become nostalgic about them. What we were responding to was the progressive urge.

And so that has always been a primary drive, in terms of my relationship with comics. I don't have any strong nostalgic associations with comics. I'm not going to rule out that there might be the odd sort of nostalgic maggot riding around somewhere deep in my heart, but, by and large, I don't have a nostalgic attachment with comics anymore.

The thing that has survived is that I am still strongly committed to the idea of progressive comic books, in whatever way that is, whether it's in terms of the story telling, the form, the content–the ones that are pushing the envelope. And that is what seems to me to be lacking in comics at the moment.

There doesn't seem to be an awful lot of experimentation going on. There doesn't even seem to be a really big desire to do anything with the form. And again, this is not a blanket criticism by any means. You can still see people like, say, Dan Clowes. The last couple of works by him that I have seen has been making some quite bold experiments with his story telling.

But, by and large, I see a lot of people who seem to have settled into... well, charitably, into a sort of work which they enjoy; but, perhaps less charitably, into a kind of rut. And this is, by no means, something that necessarily happens to all creators.

One of the people that I admire most in this entire industry is Robert Crumb, who has, throughout his extraordinarily long creative life, continued to progress and to change and to adapt. And yet, he has always remained true to himself. It can be done. Look at Robert Crumb.

Look at Will Eisner. He's somebody who, until his death, was looking for his next idea, the next way to tell a story. He was still evolving his storytelling, his ideas. I don't see that. I don't see that in a lot of the industry, and I don't really even see a desire for that. I would think that most people seem to settle for a lot less.

The tone of a lot of mainstream comics these days wouldn't seem out of place for the late 80s. There's a kind of post-*Watchmen*, post-Dark Knight cynicism that is present in them that doesn't even particularly seem to have evolved much since the 1980s. And we're talking a quarter of a century now. I know it's a bit startling to hear it put like that, but the 1980s was twenty-five years ago.

I'd just like to see some more healthy signs of growth, to feel that there were people out there who were still trying to progress.

With the ABC books, we tried to maintain quite a strong progressive thrust from the beginning right through to the end. One of the last books to come out from ABC was Promethea issue 32, which has got to be the most complex thing that I've ever done, and probably the most radical approach to the comic strip form that I've ever employed.

Although, that said, to follow on from that there is, of course, *The Black Dossier*, which is something so unusual that I'm not even sure it's a comic book anymore.

Yes, parts of it are a comic book. But it expanded to include two or three other media, and it's a bumper bundle of fun and entertainment. But, it's not all comics by any means. Comics are a part of the package, but it's something bigger than that. I'm not sure exactly what it is, but everybody will like it.

But, I don't see an awful lot of progressive moves being made by people. I don't see anything that's very daring. And, particularly at the moment, with America in a kind of an unusual state even by American standards, it's...

America seems to be going through this kind of thing that America seems to do about every 25 years. [Laughter] Nobody else in the world can understand why they're doing it. Like you get McCarthy, or you get Vietnam, the Iran Contra, you know?

BB: And Watergate, of course.

AM: Watergate, yeah, or the current Bush administration. But, I've got to say this latest one is perhaps one of the most worrying; if only because I don't see any voices being raised in protest. This is somebody who is doing things that, if Richard Nixon had done them and you'd caught him, you would have taken him out and shot him. And the mood seems to have changed so that the current administration can be caught being blatant about the things that it's doing, and nobody minds. Or nobody is prepared to say that they mind.

Like I say, I came into comics in the 60s, and the people that I admired more than anybody in the medium back then, it was the American underground artists. Hell, I'm getting married to one of them later in the year! [Laughter] That's dedication.

But they were doing stuff that was fearless, and brilliant, and necessary. If you want to look back at great cartoonists in the past, and have a look at people like [James] Gilray, a scathing scatological satirist who was completely unafraid of taking on George III, and every minister in the country, in these kind of incredibly vicious, witty, wounding portraits that were also, incidentally, works of art. Where are the Gilrays of today, now that we need them?

There is an unavoidable political element in life. And if art reflects life, or has got any relationship to life, then surely there must be an unavoidable political element in art. I'm not saying that every piece has to be a piece of political polemic, but that all of us have a political standpoint, surely, just as we all have an emotional standpoint, and an intellectual standpoint.

We can't just pretend that this has nothing to do with us. Sadly, the response from comics over this last four or five years to what is actually happening in the world seems, to me, to have been particularly lame, with very notable exceptions–people like Joe Sacco, people like Peter Kuper. You know, people who also are actually speaking their mind.

BB: Right. Guys like Ted Rall, Tom Tomorrow.

AM: Yes, yes. And there's...

I've forgotten the guy's name, but he is a kind of minimalist genius that started up a strip on his computer just using clip art of men answering the phone in offices, with obscene word balloons that were basically incredibly funny, bilious outpourings of rage against the state of civil liberties in America and the ongoing war against terror. They were collecting in a book called Get Your War On, which also was very, very funny.

BB: Right. David Rees. Great stuff.

AM: So, yeah, these people are great, the people who are actually saying something that is coherent. On the other hand, a lot of the comic industry's response to 9/11 was embarrassing.

After September 11th happened, a large number of the people that I know over there were phoning me up to either ask me to contribute some tribute or to a benefit book. And there were a number of people phoning me up just to hear what I thought of it all, to try and get some sort of sense of what was happening, by calling on me in my capacity as a "Wise Old Sage Who Knows Everything." Regardless, back to the tributes.

When Marvel asked me to do one, I said that yes, I would, on the understanding that I didn't want to be in any books that were going to have superheroes in them, because I didn't think that it was appropriate to have a tribute to 9/11 that was advertising your company's characters.

If you want to do a tribute to 9/11 then do something that actually relates to that event. Don't just show a picture of Captain America or Superman having a good cry. That's banal. So, I agreed to do something for them with Dave Gibbons, and they assured me that there weren't going to be any super heroes in it.

But, apparently, that was just to get me to agree to do something, because it had got all sorts of ridiculous superhero pictures all over it when it came out. And none of them were actually saying anything other than "Isn't this terrible?" Well, yeah. Of course it's terrible. It's always terrible when you have a large part of your city and a lot of your population killed in a sudden act of aerial violence.

The thing is that the public, in the rest of the world, we have kind of got the idea of that by now. Ever since Guernica, probably almost everywhere else in the world, apart from America, have been relatively used to being bombed. And, yes, it is always upsetting. Of course it is.

But, at the end of the day, without wishing to appear brutal, on September the 11th 2001 you lost a couple of buildings and a few thousand people. There's other people who've had it far worse, and sometimes at the hands of America. After all, New York didn't get nuked, did it?

It seems that there is some quite big conflict in the America psyche about 9/11 and all the terrible things that have happened since then. And what art is for–any form of art, but especially a fast, reactive form like comics–what art is for is to address this sort of stuff. Otherwise it's for nothing, or it's for nothing other than making money–and not even making money for the artists, but making money for the people who are handling the publishing, as you observed.

What I want is an art form that is full of ideas, and an art form which has actually got some purpose in the world. Like when I was doing Promethea. Yes, I was aware that I had to tell a story that was at least enough like a kind of magical super heroine adventure story to attract the reader's attention. But, I also wanted to pass on information that I thought was important to help people with their lives. I didn't want to preach it, but I just wanted to make it available to those who were interested. So I try to put a certain amount of content into nearly everything I do, even if it's just some little satire story in Tomorrow Stories. Then I at least try to make it a satire with a point to it, that does have some relevance. Because, otherwise, the only purpose is to shift units, which is kind of a bore, and that is not what I wanted for the comics industry.

I wanted a medium of ideas that was trying to find new things to say to keep up with our constantly changing times, one that was trying to find new ways in which to say them; that was experimenting with the form, that was trying out different things, and that was not simply a kind of, like I say, a pumpkin patch that was completely dependent upon Hollywood, or the film industry, for its survival.

That's what I thought we were moving towards, from my earliest, fourteen-year-old convention days. And then, when I actually found myself working within the industry, I was still as committed to those ideals as I've ever been.

When I was doing Warrior over here, with all the people that were working on that magazine, that was the feeling in the air; that was the buzz. "We're changing something, we're pushing things forward."

When I was doing *Watchmen* there was that same electricity–at least between me and Dave. "This is new. We are doing something new here that we've never done before, and that people have never seen before. This is really exciting. This is what it's all about!" I had the same feeling when I was doing *From Hell*, when I was doing *Lost Girls*, when I've been doing all of my more progressive books, and it's something that I...

Perhaps I'm being uncharitable; perhaps I'm just jaded; or perhaps

And my actual work in comics in the future will probably be very limited. It will be limited to the stuff that I am passionate about and the stuff that I own, which will include *The League of Extraordinary Gentlemen*, the forthcoming *Lost Girls*, and any other pieces that I come out with.

my standards are way too high–but they are my standards, and only my standards—but I feel that comics is a very lackluster affair these days. Now, I'm saying that is not without notable exceptions. There are some people--people like Harvey Pekar, who will always be good, and will always be true to himself. Still, there're an awful lot of people out there who seem to have stopped trying and, perhaps, were never as committed to progress as I might have been led to believe that they were. I don't know.

I understand that not everybody wants the same things from comics as what I do. And that's perfectly all right. It's just that that leaves me without an awful lot in the medium that I feel interested in anymore. Also, I've always been fairly remote from the doings of the business. I don't attend conventions, I don't really feel part of a kind of a comic fraternity. I've got my friends in the industry, people that I trust, but I very rarely socialize, if ever.

So, I don't really feel part of the comics industry. And that would have once made me feel very sad. But, then, the comics industry isn't the comics industry that I was working towards, or wanted. It seems to equate success with how many films are going to be made this year that have got comic characters in them. That seems to be the only way in which it measures success, or fails things. It's sort of, "*Watchmen*? Yeah, a classic, a work of art, a masterpiece." If it hadn't sold, no, it wouldn't have been any of those things.

The people who were publishing it had no idea what it was. I believe that when *Watchmen* #1 was at the printer's, Paul Levitz saw for the first time it's cover and said, "What is this?" And someone explained to him that it was the cover of *Watchmen* #1, and that the book was actually at the printer's already. And he said that, if he'd have been consulted, "It would never have been allowed to go to the press with a cover like that." Because it was obviously a cover that just didn't work as a comics cover. It hadn't got anything on it; it had got the name up sideways, up one side of it; it had got a close-up of a smiley badge. And what kind of comic book cover is that? Of course, once it had come out and everyone had said, "Oh, fantastic," the design aspects of it, you know? And, of course, "That cover, it really hit me from across the other side of the comics shop. It was so different!"

Therefore, it becomes revised so that it was a work of genius from the start in DC's eyes. "Yes, of course, we always knew this is the work of genius." No, it sold. That's what you mean.

It sold. It brought you in some money. And you've still got no idea what the book was about, even now that you've brought out all of your treasury editions and commemorative editions and anniversary editions. You've got no idea what that book was about.

As for *V for Vendetta*, if that book had ever been understood by the people publishing it in the first place, then they would not have told me that the scripts for the movie were true to my book. It wasn't. It hadn't got anything to do with my book.

My book was about fascism and anarchy, neither of which word is mentioned even once in the course of that film by all accounts. I've not seen it, of course, but my spies are everywhere.

BB: What I'm getting from all that you're saying is the idea that, for most publishers, as they attain a certain size and start to become a corporation, it's almost inevitable that those working on the lower levels, the creators in this case, are going to start getting damaged.

AM: Yeah. Used as fuel rods; discarded when they're used up.

BB: Is there any way to work within that system and not just survive, but actually thrive?

AM: Well, I've been trying to for about twenty-five years. I think that– despite the fact that there was some awful good work came out of that–in terms of my efforts to reform the industry, it was largely a wasted effort. A wasted effort that I have actually spent half of my life upon. [Laughter] Not that I feel bitter. But, what I think would be the best thing for the medium, and I know that this is not a solution that anybody else is going to go for, but I think that a good insurance fire would sort a lot of this out. Burn the industry down.

Burn it down, and leave some scorched earth from which green, tender shoots could break up into the sun of a new dawn. That's a lovely thought, isn't it? But that is genuinely how I feel.

You go to a convention now, it's big business. Not the comics so much but certainly the POGs and the action figures and everything that's attached to them. And all of the comic booky television things, like Buffy, or Star Wars, or Star Trek, or these various other things that have also been booming lately. You go to a comic convention now and they're trade fairs. They're trade fairs where the industry can actually get their target audience to pay to get in and be advertised to.

I don't really see any way out of it that doesn't involve some kind of collapse, some kind of destruction that I think is probably necessary before any genuine renewal or meaningful recovery could take place.

I should imagine that that sounds like a very bleak pronouncement from the point of view of the comics industry. But I'm not really thinking about the comics industry anymore. I'm thinking about the medium.

And the medium will always survive, even if it's some kid just drawing his own comics in biro upon a jotting pad from Woolworth's and showing them to his friends--which was pretty much the way that I got into comics when I was 10.

We used to do our own little stapled super hero comics and let our friends read them for a penny each. I'm not suggesting that all comics should be done like that, of course, but, rather, that comics are very easy to do. That is one of the most wonderful things about them.

It's not like deciding that you want to get into films. You don't suddenly need a huge amount of money backing you. You don't need a massive amount of high tech equipment. You just need a pencil and a piece of paper. And, with the kind of duplicating facilities these days, with the array of print possibilities that are open to anybody who's got a computer and decent printer, it's never been easier to actually create your own comics.

For instance, over here in England, I know that Leah [Moore, his daughter] and John [Reppion], they're doing stuff like Albion and various other mainstream stuff. But I know that they're also having a real lot of fun working with the independent small press over here, which I always used to have an awful lot of fun working with when I was at the same stage in my career as they are in theirs.

I think that that's where the new growth is. It's always on the margin. The margins that are outside comics, that is always where the invigorating new life is going to come from. And I think that that has always been the case, right through comics' history, to a certain extent.

It's the mavericks who create something new. The underground artists of the 60s became giants of the field in the 80s. I, myself, came from an underground comics background, and little things done for British music papers, things like that. And I came into the field and remodeled it as best I could to suit what were my selfish purposes. And I think that that's probably always where the new energy comes from.

But I don't think that I see anything in the comics mainstream that spells anything but demise for the medium in general. I think that it's a parasitic growth upon the art form. It drains off the art form's energies.

What we were saying earlier, that the genuine creative people, they're not the ones who profit. They're the ones who, if you look at it, if you were trying to get into comics and actually took a hard look at some of your elders and betters, and what had happened to them, you surely wouldn't think, "Oh, that's the job for me! That's how I want to end up--in a nursing home somewhere, struggling to pay my fees." There's no real incentive.

I'd have to say that the best way to go at it is the Eddie Campbell approach. He's somebody who started out just doing really, really good comic strips in little self-produced fanzines that were good enough to attract the attention of people.

Yeah. Eddie, he started out just doing comics because he loved them, and he wanted to do them in exactly the way that he wanted to do them, which meant that he'd publish them himself in these inexpensive mini-comics. And the work was good enough.

Or like Chester Brown, who started out in exactly the same way. And the work was good enough that it came to the attention of people who showed it to other people, and the word of mouth reputation was really strong. And, today, we've got two marvelous talents in the field as a result of that.

Chester Brown, I think the last thing I saw by him was Louis Riel. But what, a fantastic work; original, and true to Chester, true to himself. It's something that he did because he was interested in it.

And, of course, Eddie's work is also completely true to itself, you know? He gets closer and closer to his big hero, Henry Miller, in his observations of human life, which are always so rich, and always accomplished so elegantly and interestingly.

But that strikes me as a much better way than immediately parading on the big, financially rewarding stages of the major comic companies. I don't think there's anything there. I don't think there's any future there.

BB: Also, the mainstream publishers themselves are getting to the point where they're basically microcasting, selling to a niche market, because of the nature of the distribution system used in the States and elsewhere.

AM: Yeah. So you have got a system where you get talent that has got a tiny, specific niche market that come down to a certain number of sales, and the economics just about work out. But, it's very homogenous. Comics of the moment, manga seems to have had an incredible influence on them. And not manga in the way that I used to understand the term when I first heard it twenty-five years ago, but this new form of homogenized manga.

Back then, manga, it just mean comic strip. It was just the Japanese word for comics. Whereas now, it's become stylized to the point where every character looks like a schoolgirl with huge doe-like eyes. And this is probably the preferred form of comics for most of the readership. How does that happen?

Presumably it happened because the readers were getting something from those comics that they weren't able to find in the western serial. I really don't know, but if the western material had been better, perhaps it wouldn't have been so completely overwhelmed with these manga affectations.

It just doesn't seem to me like a healthy art form. And, possibly, that is because of the ground that it's grown out of. I was saying the other night that human beings still apparently have the same salt levels in our blood as were present in the ocean when we emerged out of the water onto the beach. Well, in the same way that we still have the same salt levels in our blood as the prehistoric seas that we originated from, so, too, the ethnic balance in comics publishers remains almost exactly the same as the ethnic balance in the Mafia at the time when the comics industry emerged from it. Not a lot of Irish publishers, you know?

The comic book industry pretty much grew out of the pulp magazines that had been used as a front by prohibition mobsters wishing to import booze from Canada under cover of a consignment of pulp periodicals. The problem is that this means the industry was founded upon mobster agendas and mobster business practices, which they have not seen fit to modify across the years except in those instances where they absolutely had to.

Another thing that should be pointed out while I'm on the subject of the shortcomings of the American industry–another thing about it is that it's racist.

It's racist. It maybe doesn't even know it is, but, unless I miss my guess, I should imagine that more than fifty percent of the readers are black, or/ and non-white. And, unless I miss my guess, I should imagine that probably less than ten percent of the people working in comics are non-white. That's kind of problematic in itself before you even get on to talking about, say, the Filipino artists.

Now there's a high point in the medium's history, surely. When I first got into comics in the 80s, everyone was still talking about the Filipino artists. Wonderful people like Rudy Nebres, and all of those fantastic artists who were working twice as hard as their American counterparts, who weren't afraid to put a little bit of black in because they weren't working for color, so they'd do texturing and feathering. Alex Nino, people like that. Master storytellers, they were working for what was known at the big companies as "Filipino rates."

Maybe there is a cultural thing in America that says it is okay to hire Filipinos and pay them less than you would a white person. Maybe if that is just seen as normal in terms of getting your domestic help or something, then maybe I could understand why it happened in comics. But, it's not okay. It's pretty far from okay.

And, yes, they sorted that out when they had to. But the fact that anybody ever thought it was a good idea in the first place, it does say something about comics. And it says something that isn't particularly nice, you know?

And, yes, there's more women working in comics by now. But there's still no where near enough. And the way that women are portrayed and treated in comics is still shameful.

When I did the first issue of Tom Strong, I got all these letters in saying how brave I'd been, thanking me for how brave I'd been with this first issue of Tom Strong, and I had no idea what they were talking about. I thought, "What do they mean? I'm doing a 1930s pastiche, or what? What did I...?"

And then it struck me that there had not been a mixed marriage, let alone one that produced a mixed race child, anywhere in American comics before that point. And that was coming out in 1999, 2000. Is it just me, or is that shameful? I hadn't even thought about it. I didn't think, "Oh, I'm going to do something really radical here. I'm going to have a mixed marriage, because nobody's ever done it over there." It's something that was not even considered.

BB: It's just a plot point, and part of the story, a part of the character.

AM: Yeah. It was just, "He's on this island. The inhabitants of the island are all black. I guess that his first romantic attachment, and perhaps the strongest one, would be with a woman of the island." And, "I want him to be married, and I want him to have kids because I want it to be a sort of an old school, cozy superhero family strip," you know? It genuinely hadn't occurred to me that...

I hadn't even noticed that he was white and she was black, and I didn't expect anybody else to. No, this stuff, it's just wrong. I'm not saying that all comics are racist. You get some incredible stuff, but they're by the usual suspects, I'm ashamed to say.

You know, you get Kyle Baker and Bob Morales doing something great. But you're not going to see many of them. It's not what the industry's geared towards.

The standards are still shockingly low in all sorts of areas. The standards of behavior, the basic philosophy that the industry seems to run on, they are so September the 10th. [Laughter] They are so last century, and some of them are so century before that. Some of the business practices don't seem to have improved since the 19th Century, you know? So that, I suppose, is pretty much the way that I've come to feel about the industry.

But, like I said, it doesn't alter anything about my love of the medium. And I shall still continue to express myself in the medium, when and where I choose to. And I shall be expressing myself in other media which I probably neglected over the past twenty-five years, due to my intense involvement with comics.

It just felt like, "It's about time!" After twenty-five years in the comics industry that I wanted to help grow and progress, it's confirmed that the industry's aims are no longer mine. And I've got other things that are very important to me, that I'm sure would not be important at all to the comics industry. Like, for example, the novel that I'm doing at the moment, *Jerusalem*.

That is something that has been the sole project that I've more or less been working on for this past year. I'm about a third of the way through, so I should imagine there's another two years of intense work on it, yet. The end result will be a thousand pages.

And I doubt if it will be of any interest to the comics readership, but it is probably the best thing that I've ever done, and it's probably the most personal work that I've ever done.

BB: Where did *Jerusalem* come from?

AM: Basically, I decided that I wanted to do a second novel, but I wasn't sure about what. I had various impulses. I thought, "Do I want to do a sequel to *Voice of the Fire?*" Then I thought, "Well, no, that's stupid. But, at the same time, I do quite like the idea of writing something about Northampton, but coming at it from a different angle."

I've thought, on and off, about doing a children's book. But, because they are so trendy at the moment, I've not wanted to touch the idea with a barge pole. So, that was somewhere in the mix. And then I basically started doing some thinking about life and death. I'm past fifty now, and the mathematics of life alters when you pass fifty.

Forty is not such a big deal. But if you get to the age of fifty, then, realistically, you're at least two-thirds of the way through, aren't you? You've got, what, two decades? Three? Something like that, if you're lucky.

So you start to think about your priorities in a different way. And I'd been thinking about death, and how did I feel about it. And it occurred to me that, basically from what I understand of science, this is a fourth dimensional universe. It has four physical dimensions, one of which we perceive as the passage of time.

But time, if I understand it correctly, isn't actually passing, except in our perception of it. In fact, as far as I understand it, every moment in the universe, from its most remote past to the most distant future, is all happening at once in some permanent, eternal kind of globe of space time in which the beginning and end of the universe are both there at the same time, along with every tiny moment in between, including all those moments which made up our lives.

And this huge solid of space time is there unchangingly forever, if I understand physics correctly. That includes all the bits of it that made up our lives. They are there, unchangingly and forever. This kind of leads me to the idea of life as an endless recurrence that, if those moments of our lives are unchanging forever, then one of the things that was conspicuous about them was that we were alive and thinking during them.

If the past hasn't got anywhere to go, it's still there, isn't it? And it must just be our consciousness moving through the solid of space time that gives us the illusion of passing time. It strikes me that there really isn't any need for life after death, because life before death is, very probably, eternal. I can conceive of us just...

It's not like reincarnation. It's we are reborn into the same life over and over and over again. That is what I think could very likely be the situation. I can't think of any angles from which that is wrong, or impossible, or does not fit with current scientific theory.

And it struck me that, if such a thing was, indeed, the actual truth of our situation, then there's an interesting moral inference that can be drawn from it. And that is that, if every moment of your life is eternal, then live every moment of your life in such a way that you could be happy to live it over and over again eternally. Which doesn't sound like a bad way of living one's life. "Don't do anything that you can't live with forever." And that idea, of every moment in life being eternal, you have to admit that...

Imagine, the best moments of your life, forever. That is surely eternal reward. And the worst moments of your life, forever, is surely unending

Yeah, there are still some very notable creators within the field, but they are mainly on the margins. I have been, I think, disappointed with some of the center ring acts seen in comics lately.

damnation. I think that, probably, in this kind of proposed cosmology there is enough heaven and hell to satisfy any rabid, fundamentalist brimstone preacher. Also, it'd be kind of fair, wouldn't it? You'd have judged yourself, in effect, rather than been judged by some remote higher authority.

Anyway, it was an idea that struck me, and I started to apply it to my own life, to the lives of my family, to the neighborhood that I grew up in.

Now, the neighborhood that I grew up in is this very, very unusual neighborhood, indeed. It's a tiny, impoverished square mile of dirt known as the Boroughs in Northampton. So the Boroughs is a totally obscure place, but it's also one of the most important places, historically, in this country.

It was where King John's castle was, as mentioned in Shakespeare's play, King John. So it was where three, I believe, of the four Crusades were raised– at the corner of Andrews Road, where I was born.

The western world's first parliament was raised there in the 1300s. The first poll tax, which caused the peasants revolt over here, was raised there in the 1300s.

Philip Doddridge, the man who completely changed the Anglican Church, he did it all while he was serving as the minister at Castle Hill, in the heart of the Boroughs. He introduced non-conformism to the English Church and completely changed the church within something like twenty-five years, completely overhauled the entire Anglican Church. And on and on, this fantastic cavalcade of sometimes historically famous people, sometimes ones that weren't perhaps as famous, but were every bit as important.

There was a liberated black slave who went by the name of Black Charlie. He lived in Scarletwell Street, which is just around the corner from where my house used to be, although he was there round about 1910. I think he'd come over to the Boroughs in 1897. He rode around with a rag and bone cart towed behind his bicycle, and both the cart and the bicycle had lengths of rope instead of tires. And on his shoulder he had the brand of the slave plantation in Tennessee that he'd been liberated from in 1863. When, by my estimate, he would have been thirteen. I figure he must have been born about 1850 from the date on his death certificate.

I hadn't actually known that the plantations used to actually brand the slaves. That was a new one on me. And I found myself having to wonder at what age they did it, if he was already branded by the age of 13.

When would you brand a child?

It's funny the things you have to consider when you're writing a novel. What would be a good age to brand a child? You know, you wouldn't want to do it at two; that'd kill them, wouldn't it? But you wouldn't want to leave it too late in case they ran away, or fought back, or something.

But, yeah, he came by a circuitous route and ended up in Northampton, where he was completely accepted in the Boroughs, and was a beloved local figure. And I've mixed that in with some other true local stories.

The man who wrote Amazing Grace lived just over the border in Buckinghamshire. And there were some very interesting things about the man who wrote Amazing Grace, particularly in relation to slavery. So this is just one chapter–one chapter out of thirty-five.

So, like I've said, this book is going to be probably over a thousand pages long. It will certainly be the longest thing that I've ever done, including Swamp Thing, which I think was previously the longest thing that I'd ever actually written, in terms of the numbers of pages. This is going to be much longer than that.

And it's talking about bits from my family history. Although I've changed the names of everybody, so it's not about me, me, me. I fictionalized it. In fact, in the middle section, which takes place in Heaven, I've heavily fictionalized it. [Laughter] But, at the same time, it's based upon real events.

I did have a brother–still do, as a matter of fact–who managed to choke to death when he was three or four, and then recovered from it, surprisingly; but recovered from all of ten minutes without breathing. Which...

We were just grateful at the time. We didn't think too much about it. But, as the years wind by, you find yourself thinking about these odd little things, and wondering, "How did that happen?" So, that has provided a big part of the book.

So, yeah, it's a big novel. But, then, on the other hand, it does explain where we go when we die, which is quite ambitious, I think, for a book. And it's also got this magnificent sweep of history relating to so many different things–slavery, poverty, politics, religion, hymns, visionaries, poets and crack whores, which is what the main thing that my former neighborhood is known for at the moment. It's the red light district of the town, and is horrifically violent. It seems that there's a prostitute who's been beaten and raped down there every other week. They don't even report most of them.

This is the beloved neighborhood in which I grew up, and a place which has got history going back to Saxon times, to the 8th century.

BB: Sounds like you've got plenty of material.

AM: Yeah, that's it. I've certainly got an awful lot of material. And I'm not even having to repeat any of the stuff that I used for Voice of the Fire, even though an awful lot of that did happen in the tiny area that I'm talking about.

But, like I say, its name is *Jerusalem*. It will take me a couple of years. I've not got a publisher for it yet, and I'm not looking for one. I'm really enjoying doing this without an editor, without anybody–apart from Steve Moore, who is actually a real editor, and one of the best in the business.

He's going through and correcting my historical and grammatical errors for me. But, other than that, I'm writing exactly what I want to write. And it's very, very liberating.

BB: How have you approached writing it? Did you basically have your facts in hand and then just sat down and started writing, as you did with the ABC stuff?

AM: Pretty much. What I did was, I wrote down thirty-five smart sounding phrases that made good chapter titles. I just said, "Oh, that'd make a clever chapter title. That's kind of funny. That's kind of resonant." Then, after I got a vague idea as to what those chapters might be about, I decided to do a three-part structure for the book: beginning, middle and end.

So, I came up with three section titles and then divided up the chapter titles into three piles, if you like, according to where in the book they seemed to fit best. Then I got them into order. So I've got the plan of the book, all three sections that make it up and the thirty-five chapters that comprise those three sections. I'm probably going to have to have a prologue, an epilogue, and eleven chapters in each section. Once I'd got that, I just started writing.

And, like I say, I'm now exactly three hundred pages in, I think, after doing it for a year. I'm about a third of the way, or just over a third of the way through.

BB: Are you mainly working on paper, in longhand, before transferring it to the computer, as you used to do?

AM: No, I'm writing straight onto the machine this time. Because I find that, with comics, where I was actually drawing layouts, yeah, you do pretty much have to do it by hand. It makes more sense to just be able to draw little tiny sketches and then scribble in the dialogue next to it. But with this, I might as well just create it as I'm sitting at the screen.

I do, on a good day, about a page to two pages on a good day. I'm being very careful. I want this to be very, very good writing.

BB: A lot of time spent thinking and working out things before you put it down? Or are you putting things down and then re-writing them?

AM: Well, I probably spend a lot of time sitting there and thinking about it before I put it down, and then get it wrong anyway. Then I go back and rewrite it. Then I hand it to Steve Moore, and he points out that there're two grammatical errors and an historical error in that sentence, and I rewrite it again. So this is probably one of the more polished things of mine, although people are going to have to wait for a while before it'll see the light of day.

I'm probably actually doing more work upon it. I'm spending longer at the keyboard every day, religiously, than I was with the comics. Maybe it's taking me longer to do because it is about something that is so complex and personal. But I think it's going to be worth the wait. I think this should have a few pleasant surprises in it.

BB: Well, I was about to ask about that aspect of it, especially since you started to work in a, physically in essentially a new way, if this project had led to any surprises or discoveries?

AM: Yeah. I found out how much I love just writing, as opposed to just writing comics, which I still love. But I found out how much I love writing prose, and how much I like writing unsupervised, where I can get up to all sorts of mischief, and there's nobody to tell me not to. [Laughter]

It's great, and it feels like it's about something which is vital and important. I mean, it might not be important to anybody else in the world what happens to the tiny, run down neighborhood that I originated from. But, if I write this book correctly, then the neighborhood that I originated from will become universal. It will become the neighborhoods that we all originated from, and what happened to them, and how important they were. All of these lost districts that we emerged from, and then the work ran out, or they went downhill. Factories started buying up the houses or they built big tower blocks of flats where there used to be rows of cozy-looking streets. This is a fairly universal story, even though I am telling you about a very specific area of Northampton.

So, yeah, it feels like I'm doing something worthwhile, that I've got something of human importance in there, and something which relates to everything that's going on in the world at the moment.

Like, at the moment, somewhere just outside the one square mile of the Boroughs, there's a guy living practically under house arrest at the moment. He was the assistant of the local Labor MP Member of Parliament, a Northampton man who had got a friend, a fellow Northamptonian, who was also in the Labor Party. This other guy worked in the Foreign Office. It was in all the papers over here, this guy that worked in the foreign office had intercepted...

There'd been a piece of paper that had come to his attention, which was a transcript of a conversation between your beloved leader, George Bush, and our beloved leader, Tony Blair. And apparently they were discussing whether to bomb Al Jazeera. [Laughter] I mean, "Why not?" Which, just to recap, is a television station, is a civilian target, and is in a country that we are not actually at war with. So proposing to bomb it is sort of a war crime, you know? Not to harp on about this sort of stuff, but it is. It's a war crime.

And, apparently, this guy thought, "I don't know if I could just pass this on and just not say anything about it. I think I ought to alert somebody." So, he got in touch with his friend in Northampton who was the assistant of the local MP. The local MP had seen the e-mail, and had realized that he would probably be on the Special Branch's list as an accomplice if he didn't report it.

So he reported it, and yeah, these guys are still awaiting trial. Which has become a little bit confused, because the Foreign Office at first denied that such a conversation had ever taken place between the two leaders; and then, inadvertently, another part of the Foreign Office admitted that, in fact, they did have tapes of such a conversation. Though it's going to be a bit tricky as to what they actually prosecute these people for.

This is happening right in the Boroughs at the moment. And it's kind of, "Yeah, everywhere in the world is connected with everywhere else in the world." It's too small a world these days, and we're all wired up together. So I figured that by talking about a tiny, insignificant smear of a place like the Boroughs, I've probably got a pretty good chance of ending up talking about everything–by being very, very specific and becoming, as a result, universal. That's the plan anyway.

BB: Reflecting the microcosmic in the macrocosmic, and vice versa?

AM: Yeah, yeah.

BB: Jumping back just a bit, I was wondering what makes Steve Moore such a good editor?

AM: Steve Moore was an editor when he was sixteen, working in the comics industry over here in this country. Now, these were juvenile comics, and they were intended for an audience of eleven- to thirteen-year-old boys, but the editorial standards that Steve was taught to adhere to were old school, and they were stringent.

Steve is somebody who's ferociously intelligent. He's probably one of the most intelligent people that I know. He's a fellow of the Royal Asiatic Society. He's a polymath who understands nearly everything about Eastern culture, has a tremendous grasp of classical history, and is a really penetrating thinker–incredibly level-headed, with an incredible imagination.

And he's somebody that's probably been my closest friend since I was about fourteen. He's the person who taught me how to write comics by his example. Also, and this is perhaps something that makes him such a good editor, while he started out as an editor, he was most interested in writing himself. As soon as he got the opportunity to move into writing, he did so. And so he's not working from a position of being somebody who doesn't actually have any abilities within the field that they are advising other people on. Steve is a good writer on his own account.

He's also one of the very few editors who would dare to suggest changes in something that I'd written. Which is all very good for my sense of ego, but perhaps is not necessarily the best thing for my writing. Most editors wouldn't presume that they knew better than me. Whereas Steve can, with justification, presume so.

He's known me for a long time. He knows how sloppy I am. He knows how I'll just kind of put a date in that I think I've remembered right, but haven't bothered to check. And that's the exact opposite of him. He's precise, meticulous, and so he's doing a fantastic job on *Jerusalem*. He's covering it with red ink.

And he's being as pedantic as he possibly can be, which is what I told him to be. I said, "Just give this the most rigorous and hostile editing that you can come up with," and he saw clumsy phrases, and then picked me up on them. [Laughter] And that's what he's doing. I've only actually gone over about five pages of his revisions to the first chapter thus far. I just did a little bit of that today.

It's going to be a bit of work, doing the revisions, but it's not going to be–thanks to the kind of suggestions that Steve's made–it's not going to be blinding me, nor take the crippling extra six months of labor that I thought it was going to be.

So, that's why Steve's really good [at editing]. He was the person who instructed me on how to get into comics, and he was the person who instructed me on how to get into magic, probably two of the most important moves in my life. And he's a tremendously influential person in his own right.

Like I say, without him, British comics fandom might not have existed. And if British comics fandom hadn't existed, then almost none of the currently favored British comics artists or writers would have existed.

So, yeah, for my purposes, Steve Moore is the best.

BB: Well, for those fans of your comics, there is some good news, because you still have a couple projects coming out. Why don't we start with *The Black Dossier* before moving on to *Lost Girls*?

AM: *The Black Dossier* will be the last thing to come out with ABC. Kevin [O'Neill] is, I believe, at the moment 41 pages away from the end of it. So, yes, I expect it later this year. And the stuff that he's done so far is absolutely magnificent. It is the best. Even though it is not volume 3 of *The League of Extraordinary Gentlemen*, it's probably the best collection of *The League of Extraordinary Gentlemen* yet to appear. He's got so much in it.

BB: How would you describe it?

AM: Imagine a source book that has got lots of interesting snippets from here and there in *The League of Extraordinary Gentlemen*'s three or four hundred year history. But, these are presented in some unusual ways. For example, when we want to talk about the founding of *The League of Extraordinary Gentlemen*, which involved Prospero, then we include a lost Shakespeare folio for a play called Fairy's Fortunes Founded, which Shakespeare commenced to write in 1616, which was the year of his death, and thus never completed. So we have got the opening scenes of Fairy's Fortunes Founded reproduced in the manner of a Shakespeare folio as part of *The Black Dossier*, fully illustrated and featuring some pretty good Shakespeare, if I say so myself.

And when we're detailing the 18th century League, the Gulliver group, then this is done in the form of a sequel to John Cleland's Fanny Hill, it "Being the Further of the Adventures of a Woman of Pleasure," with lots of text and full page illustrations, like in the illustrated Fanny Hill that the Marquis Von Bayros illustrated. So, there're those things. And there's lots of things that you might expect in a source book, like a really neat double page cutaway of the Nautilus. There's a twenty-five page comic strip history done in the style of those great old full color English comic strips that we used to have in Boy's World, or things like that; stuff that was painted, like Dan Dare was painted.

This history is, essentially, a twenty-five page "Life of Orlando," which tells the entire life of Orlando from his birth in the City of Thebes in 1190 B.C. And then, basically in the life of Orlando, we give the timeline for the entire *The League of Extraordinary Gentlemen*'s world, up to the Second World War. And we've got every famous fictional character and event that you've ever heard of in there.

It turns out that Orlando has slept with absolutely everybody. And the ones he hasn't slept with, he's waged terrible war upon. If he was a he at the time, you know? He's posed for the Mona Lisa, and he's fought at Troy. He was personally responsible for the Renaissance, he believes. That was a lot of fun. But, that was just twenty-five pages.

There's a Beat Generation novel, allegedly inspired by the activities of The League in America during the 1950s, as written by Sal Paradise, who was the surrogate for Jack Kerouac that appeared in On the Road. And it's a Beat novel called The Crazy Wide Forever, which has got The League teaming up with Sal Paradise and Dean Moriarty against the villainous Dr. Sax, from another Kerouac book, as he was a kind of cross between Fu Manchu, The Shadow, and William Boroughs. So, yeah, we've got Dr. Sax in there.

There's an immense amount of stuff in the Dossier. A prospectus of London, features upon previous versions of *The League of Extraordinary Gentlemen*, Les Hommes Mysterieux from France, and Der Zweilicht-helden from Germany. There's an account of The Surrogate League that British Intelligence tried to put together in the 1950s, and which was a complete disaster. There's everything that you could ever want to know about any incarnation of The League. And this is the source book material; this is the actual Black Dossier.

And, wrapped around that and running through that, there are these very lengthy sections of comic strip which tell the story of *The League of Extraordinary Gentlemen*, such as it is, basically retrieving *The Black Dossier* from British Intelligence in 1958. They basically steal *The Black Dossier* that has got all of these things that British Intelligence know about *The League of Extraordinary Gentlemen* contained in it. Members of The League break into British Intelligence in 1958, steal *The Black Dossier*, and then try to escape from the country while being pursued by a trio of deadly British agents, who are trying to get them and the Dossier back.

And, as you might expect with The League, there is nobody who appears anywhere in these books who is not somebody that you probably should have heard of or heard about from literature, or from films or comics or from some other cultural source.

But, I don't want to tell you who's in it. For one thing, as I'm sure you can imagine, the closer we get to the present day in *The League of Extraordinary Gentlemen*, the more intricate the dance around the minor matters like copyright has to be. Victorian characters are fair game. They're all public domain. Even so, you occasionally get someone like Sax Rohmer who, I believe, didn't have the decency to die until sometime in the 1940s or 50s, which meant that we couldn't use Dr. Fu Manchu in The League. So we just used an oriental mastermind who was known as the Doctor, and who was controlling Limehouse, but everybody knew who it was.

And that's the technique that we're approaching some of the characters with in this Dossier. There are some very famous characters in there who we can't actually spell out who they are, but everybody will know who they're supposed to be, because we make it completely obvious. We do everything but spell it out.

And the actual material in that comic strip is much, much more interesting than the actual wonderful material in the Dossier itself. It's got this sort of fascinating flight across England, touching upon a number of interesting English fictional characters of the 1950s, and, it ends with probably the most spectacular sixteen pages you have ever seen in any comic. I'm saying this before Kevin's actually drawn them, but, I know what they're going to be like. There are a lot of little extras that we put in this, as well.

BB: How about the multi-media aspects of *The Black Dossier*? What can you say about that part of the project?

AM: Well, part of the book, which is set in 1958, remember, deals with the residual influence of George Orwell's Big Brother Government. That book was originally set in 1948. But the publisher said, "Well, George, nobody's going to understand this. Let's change the last two numbers around, and we'll say it's happening in the future." And so, instead of being called 1948, it was called 1984. So, by the time our book opens in 1958, the

Big Brother Government has already been over for a number of years. So we've got a lot of references to Orwell's world, and we tie that into our world in a way that makes perfect sense.

As one of the little extra giveaways, we've got a book produced by Pornsec, which, in Orwell's book, they're working for the Ministry of Truth, the Ministry of Propaganda, and they produce these little pornographic comics. And so, one of the giveaways is an eight-page Tijuana Bible, as dreamed up by Orwell's Thought Police. So it's Thought Police pornography. And that is something that will fall into your lap like subscription cards when you open the book.

There is a pair of 3-D goggles that will be included as well, that will be necessary for one section of the book–quite an important section of the book, actually.

And there is a 45 [RPM] vinyl single that is supposedly by a 1950s band on a 1950s American record label, both of which are fictitious, but which are taken from other sources. That's part of the fun of The League, you know? The band is called "Eddie Enrico and His Hawaiian Hotshots," which, I believe, were mentioned very briefly by Thomas Pynchon in his excellent The Crying of Lot 49. But it's double-sided, it's a single with two sides. One side of which is "Immortal Love," and the other side of which is "Home with You," which are kind of League-themed 1950s pop songs.

And so, yeah, there'll be a lot of little extras in this. It's going to be a very handsomely produced volume. And, like I say, Kevin's about 41 pages away from the end now.

BB: Just out of curiosity, who did the music?

AM: Who did the music? It was me and Tim Perkins, pretending to be a 50s American rock and roll band. I've discovered, at this late stage in my life, that I am, in fact, an Elvis impersonator. But you'll have to wait and listen for yourself, you know? [His voice assumes an Elvis Presley-like drawl] "Uh huh, thank you very much."

So there'll be a lot of little goodies, because me and Kevin like that. We like having lots of nice little things in there. It reminds us of British comics of our youth, where there were always these kind of cheap giveaways

PROMETHEA

America's Best Comics®

32
april

wildstorm.com

DIRECT SALES

03211

7 61941 22058 1

$3.95 us $6.00 can

universe

With the ABC books, we tried to maintain quite a strong progressive thrust from the beginning right through to the end. One of the last books to come out from ABC was Promethea issue 32, which has got to be the most complex thing that I've ever done, and probably the most radical approach to the comic strip form that I've ever employed.

included. But we've got some quite expensive giveaways in this one.

BB: And porn, too!

AM: Absolutely. It is 1984 Newspeak totalitarian porn, so it's kind of depressing, but also kind of funny. [Laughter] It's George Orwell's 1984, told as an 8-page tale in a Tijuana Bible pornographic comic strip, which is kind of funny and dreadful at the same time. But that's just a minor bauble to fall into the reader's lap.

So, yeah, that's *The Black Dossier*. And, the other thing that will be coming out very, very soon is *Lost Girls*, which is probably one of the most...

It's a comic book that I've been working on with Melinda for about the past sixteen or seventeen years now. And it's probably one of the most important works I've ever done. We've got it absolutely perfect, as far as we know. It's at the printers now. So we'll finally get some feedback, which is good, as long as it's not lynch mobs or squinting peasants carrying pitchforks and torches. [General laughter] After fifteen years, we're going to be very, very glad to get some reaction to this, and we think that the reaction will probably be quite positive. We're very proud of it. It's certainly not like anything else that's ever appeared before.

This is not just different to any kind of erotica that's ever appeared in comics, this is different to any kind of erotica that has ever appeared. And the history of erotica, especially, goes a lot, lot further back than the history of comics. It's got everything. It's clever. It's allusive. It's referencing all these other prominent people from the world of erotica. All these artists and writers who are often overlooked, or at least that part of their work which was erotic is often overlooked, or shoved under the carpet, because it embarrasses us, even at this juncture of the 21st century.

So, it is a book that's about sex. And it's about pornography, as well as being pornography. But it has themes. It has an idea behind it. It has got all the things that you would expect to find in any kind of novel. But it's also got Melinda's fantastic artwork, which is all that you could expect to find in an art gallery. But these are combined into one work, and I think that this will be some of the very best erotica, and perhaps some of the most ambitious, that has ever been produced anywhere in the world.

We'll see what kind of reaction there is to it. But, like I say, I think it'll probably be a strong one, one way or the other. I don't think there'll be many people ignoring this, you know?

BB: What makes it one of the most important works you've ever done?

AM: Well, for one thing, it is one of the only times that I've extensively worked with a woman. That is very different, given that nearly all of the other people that I've worked with are male. So that has given a different dynamic to it.

Also, the fact that me and Melinda are involved together. It's the first time I've ever worked on a really big project with somebody that I was emotionally involved with. That gives it something different, so that it becomes something that is very much involved with me and Melinda, and our relationship. So that is a big part of it.

Also, it's because of the subject matter, and the seriousness in which we are treating the subject matter. It's like we, as a culture, have an awful--and, I'm not just talking about England; I'm talking about most of the western world, and, perhaps, most of the world--but we, as a species, seem to have an awful lot of problems with our sexual imaginations, and with our sex lives. We seem to be haunted by all sorts of fears and phantoms of lingering guilt or shame, and an inability to actually talk about this stuff with a straight face.

And yet, it is something so central to all of our lives. We all think about it. Everybody does. We know we do. So why do we pretend that we don't? Is it because we think it makes us a look a bit more civilized? No, not really. A child-like embarrassment over sex is not really a mark of civilization.

So, we've decided to treat this as if sex was actually an enjoyable part of the human experience. I know that's going to sound crazy, and from left field, but we've treated it as if sex is actually something that's enjoyable, and it's something that a lot of people spend their time exercising their imaginations upon. And as if this is okay and normal, and is all right, and is just a human thing that people do. That's the point that we've started from. And then we've decided [to answer questions like], "Can we make this beautiful? Can we make this intelligent? Can we make this informative? Can we make some moral point with this?"

Also, it's a very well-timed book, at least in the sense that, yes, it is a passionate argument for the freedom of the sexual imagination. That is true.

But it is also just as passionate an argument against war; against war as a complete failure of any sort of imagination. And war as a perversion of the sex drive, where young men often–always, predominantly young men, but increasingly the young women, too–at the age of their lives when they should be putting all of their energy into having sex, instead get that erotic energy perverted and turned into a Thanatic drive. They're sent over to some remote part of the world to kill and/or be killed. But, you don't even have to evoke names like Wilfred Owen to talk about the losses to culture that any wars brings.

He's just one of the famous poets that we know got completely wasted in the First World War. I mean, some of those kids are eighteen or nineteen. They haven't written their first book yet.

So how many geniuses, how many Shakespeares, how many Mozarts have we sent over to some foreign hellhole to get their brains spattered over the side of a trench, that we've never even heard about? The ones who could have gone on to cure cancer, you know, or who could have cured the sadness in our souls?

We send them over there because there was a bit of territory that we wanted, or there was some fuel that we wanted, some money. Something that we thought that we'd like, or which our leaders thought that they'd like, and so we decided that it was worth sacrificing a potentially endless number of us to acquire it.

So, yeah, *Lost Girls* is passionately anti-war, every bit as much as it is passionately pro-sex. And it's coming out at a good time. If this had come out when we first started doing it, it wouldn't have been so stark in contrast with its times. But today, where we seem to be in an almost permanent state of war, then I think it's going to be very, very timely.

And it talks about art, and it talks about music, and it talks about sex, and it talks about politics, and it talks about history. It's got the first performance in comics, as far as I know, of Igor Stravinsky's Rite of Spring, and the first time that I've ever attempted, with Melinda, to actually reproduce a ballet in comic book form. How do you do the music, for example?

But, yeah, like I say, it's wonderful. We've seen the page proofs, and it is a wonderful-looking piece of design work. I think people are going to have their breath taken away, if only by the artwork. I'm not saying anything about my story. But just the artwork, alone, I think is very, very arresting. And to have artwork of this delicacy and beauty applied to sex, you wonder why no one's done it before. You know what I mean?

You wonder why every piece of pornography, whether it's in comic books, or in films, or whatever, is lit as if it's for brain surgery, so that you can see every pore. I've not got anything against realism, but I'm quite fond of romance, as well as realism. So this is romantic hardcore sex, and beautifully rendered, which does something to change the nature of the experience.

Also, this is a very, very big book, or it's three very big hardback books. So, it's not really one-handed reading material. You're going to need both hands for this; that's just a warning, to the buyer.

But, yeah, that's going to be coming out in a few months, and it's going to be wonderful. That is something we've both been waiting for, for a very long time, and we're both very excited about it. And we'll see what the reaction is.

It's a book which is easily as complicated and as rich as Watchmen. In terms of what Watchmen did for superhero stories, this does the same for erotica, if that gives any kind of grasp of what we're trying to do here. Well, that's the only thing the two works have got in common–a similar ambition and complexity and grace of execution.

But this is actually about something that's much more important than superheroes. Superheroes aren't real, and sex is. Superheroes do not affect our lives, and sex does. [Laughter] I mean, sex is how we got here! You'd think that someone would have done a serious book about it by now. *Lost Girls* is our attempt at just that.

Then, beyond that, there're a couple of my poetic works [being adapted to comics]. I know that Melinda is going to be working on the William Blake piece that I did, Angel Passage. So, Melinda is stretching watercolor paper at the moment, and getting that project sorted out. And I think Jose Villarrubia is going to be doing an adaptation of a piece off my first CD [The Moon and Serpent Grand Egyptian Theatre of Marvels]. There was a section of that which was called The Book of Copulations, which was pretty hard core magic–on the edge, very raw. And Jose has just asked me the other day if I would mind if he adapted that, and I happily agreed to it.

So, there's those two pieces, which don't actually involve much work upon my part, because I've already done my work. But I shall be watching over them with great interest.

And then there is, finally, the continuation of *The League of Extraordinary Gentlemen*, which will come out from a kind of conglomerate of Top Shelf and Knockabout, handling it in America and England, respectively. We figured that we want to approach this one differently, this volume three. For one thing, we think it'd make more sense if, instead of doing six thirty-two page comics, we do three sixty-four or seventy-two page books that will each tell a complete story in themselves, while building up into a three-part narrative, so that it will be kind of a modular approach to the storytelling. That way, if there is a gap between issue #1 and issue #2, it won't matter because, realistically, they're going to take as long as they take, anyway. But we think that it would be better if we've got a whole narrative chunk satisfyingly concluded within each book, so that the readers aren't left on tenterhooks between issues, and yet will still provide a satisfying experience when they read all three stories collected together.

As for the nature of the story, it's going to be unusual for The League in that it's going to take place in three separate time periods. The first book will take place in 1910, around the date of the coronation of King George V. The second book will take place in 1968, at one of the free festivals that they used to have in Hyde Park over here in the hippie period, and will be

Bill Baker Presents...

featuring some characters from the 60s in the usual mix. And there'll be a story line running through all of these that will build up to the third book, which takes place in 2008, and is a kind of apocalyptic conclusion to the story line that's been building up through the background of the first two volumes. So, yeah, that will be volume three of The League.

And, after that, me and Kevin would probably like to get on with some individual stories, some Tales of *The League of Extraordinary Gentlemen* that could just focus upon, say, one character.

Orlando is a very tempting character to do a one-off special based upon, especially after you see the way that we've treated him/her in The Dossier. And there's also another character that we introduce to The League in *The Black Dossier*; the first black character in The League, and, of course, a controversial one. But he is also such a fantastic character discovery that we're very tempted to do a special based upon his adventures.

So that's the rough plan at the moment. But this might be changed at any point, you know? That's the nature of plans, as I'm sure Donald Rumsfeld is aware. But, at least for the moment, what we intend to do is to go for a three-issue volume three that will be issued as three separate seventy-two page comics, which will then be gathered up into a complete collection.

And then, after that, like I say, maybe we'll just focus upon "Tales of *The League of Extraordinary Gentlemen*" for a year or two before we do another story with the whole bunch. We don't know. We kind of take it as we find it.

But we're both very excited to be doing these outside the auspices of DC Comics, because I think that me and Kevin are both feeling pretty much the same way about how we were being treated. So, yeah, we've got a spring in our step. There's a future that's full of wonderful possibilities and I'm looking forward to exploring it as thoroughly as I can.

BB: In our past conversations, when we touched upon some troubling situation or problem one of us was encountering, you'd often conclude with an observation which has provided me with a surprising amount of comfort–once I got over the Existential terror it invoked. [General laughter] So, I was wondering if it's still true that, "None of this will matter in 250 million years," as I've heard you say in the past, or has your position on that matter changed somewhat?

AM: That is true. But, the thing is that, if I'm right with this new *Jerusalem* hypothesis, it matters eternally now, you know? I'm not sure if that will undo all the comfort that my previous remark brought to you. [Laughter]

But I'm now of the opinion that every moment matters incredibly. And it matters eternally. It's not that it will matter in 250 million years, but it's just that this particular moment is eternally here. And so it matters eternally.

If I'm right–and, like I say, I haven't been able to think of a way in which I'm wrong yet–that doesn't really help you. But, if I was having to put money on it, I'd put it on me, you know?

I think that everything matters. I think that the most tiny, little thing–the most tiny, unnoticeable little thing–matters. That is the hypothesis that I'm putting forward in *Jerusalem*. It all matters. It's all crucial. Even if we can't see why it matters, you know?

But, if looked at from a fourth dimensional perspective that was outside of time, I'm sure the pattern would be a lot more apparent to us, which is also one of the things that I suggest in this book. It really does reflect the view of life that has come to me during my maturity, or what I hope is my maturity. If looked at from a fourth dimensional perspective that was outside of time, the apparently random events of our lives might have a pattern that was meaningful. They might even have a pattern that was beautiful, even the stretches that seemed ugly when we were living through them. All our personal disasters may have, all the time, been graceful brush-strokes in some unimaginable and transcendent work of art.

The preceding conversation took place on May 8th, 2006, between the hours of 12:15 and 3:50 pm EST [USA]. There were two brief interruptions during the taping, resulting in an interview of approximately 3 hours and 40 minutes duration. This text has been both proofed and approved by Alan Moore.

– Bill Baker

Where to find books by Alan Moore...

An incredibly prolific author, Alan Moore has worked for a wide variety of publishers over the past 25-plus years, making a complete listing of his published works a book-length project in its own right. Also, and quite surprising for a creator this perennially popular, a fair amount of his work is currently out of print and only available in single-issue format from the back issue bins of comic shops.

Fortunately, there are a fair number of collected editions, original graphic novels and adaptations of his work, in print and readily available via independent and chain book stores, as well as comic book shops, to satisfy all but the most fanatical of readers. Below you'll find a short listing of the major publishers offering work by Moore and his many collaborators, along with some short notations to help guide your search.

AMERICA'S BEST COMICS, LLC

7910 Ivanhoe# 438, La Jolla, CA 92037, USA
www.DCcomics.com/WildStorm
ABC, a subsidiary of WildStorm Productions which is owed by DC Comics, published the majority of Alan Moore's later commercial comics, including the entire ABC line of books–including Promethea, Tomorrow Stories, Tom Strong, The Forty-Niners and Top Ten–as well as the first two volumes of the creator-owned The League of Extraordinary Gentlemen.

CHECKER BOOK PUBLISHING GROUP

17 N. Main Street, Suite 31, Centerville, OH 45459, USA
www.CheckerBPG.com
Checker publishes several trades featuring a solid sampling of Moore's mainstream superhero work from the '90s, including Supreme, an award-winning, critically acclaimed and incredibly entertaining Superman pastiche that readily transcends the genre's limitations.

DC COMICS

1700 Broadway, New York, NY 10019, USA
www.DCcomics.com
DC published much of Moore's seminal work during the 80s and very early 90s, including V for Vendetta, Watchmen and a truly phenomenal Swamp Thing run, as well as various short runs, single issues, specials and one shots. All of Moore's shorter work for the company, including The Killing Joke graphic novella, has been compiled into a single trade paperback, DC Universe: The Stories of Alan Moore. This means, essentially, that almost all of Moore's important commercial work from this period is now readily available. Much of it, especially Watchmen and his Swamp Thing run, is essential reading for any who wish to be considered serious connoisseurs or students of the medium. Also, these books are generally acknowledged as exceptionally good places to begin reading Moore's work.

TITAN BOOKS

144 Southwark St, London SE1 OUP, England
www.2000ADonline.com
Publishers of some of the earliest of Moore's comics work, these folks have also been pretty good about keeping most of these books–including The Ballad of Halo Jones, The Complete D.R. & Quinch and Skizz–in print and available. Solid, entertaining and often thought-provoking, the work from this early period also offers the astute reader a chance to chart Moore's growth as a writer, while learning a host of subtle but important lessons in the storyteller's craft.

TOP SHELF PRODUCTIONS

P. O. Box 1282, Marietta, GA 30061-1282, USA
www.topshelfcomix.com
Publishers of a wide variety of cartoonists, this independent press has fostered and developed strong relationships with a number of creators, including Eddie Campbell and Alan Moore. So it makes perfect sense that this imprint has been the publisher of choice for much of Moore's more recent experimental comics and prose projects, such as From Hell and Lost Girls, Voice of the Fire and The Mirror of Love. As Moore himself notes in this very book, this is the imprint which will be releasing much of his future comics work, including all future League of Extraordinary Gentlemen adventures. [Note: Some of these new projects will be co-published with Knockabout, an English independent publisher of relatively recent vintage.]

Alan Moore is an award winning author of comics and short stories, prose and graphic novels, plays and other entertainments. He is also one of the most celebrated and influential creators to have ever worked in the comics industry. He's written any number of highly acclaimed graphic novels over the course of his quarter century career, including From Hell, The League of Extraordinary Gentlemen, Promethea and, most recently, the epic erotic masterpiece, Lost Girls. He first came to prominence in the 1980s with his work on, among other titles, a revival of the British comic character Marvelman (published as Miracleman in the US). This notice lead to his being offered work by various mainstream and independent American comic companies. Moore made the most of this opportunity by scripting a now-legendary run of revolutionary stories featuring DC Comics icons like Batman, Superman and the Swamp Thing, as well as a string of original extended tales, including V for Vendetta and Watchmen, books that are now widely recognized as seminal masterpieces of the medium and important cornerstones of the modern graphic novel market.

Alan Moore resides in his native England, surrounded by books, friends and family members. Presently, Alan is working on Jerusalem, his second prose novel, and eagerly awaiting the day when his fiancée, the gifted comic artist, illustrator and painter Melinda Gebbie, makes an honest man of him.

Bill Baker is a veteran entertainment and comics journalist, and the author of two nonfiction books, Alan Moore Spells It Out (2005) and Alan Moore's Exit Interview (2007). Over the past eight years, Bill regularly contributed interviews and feature stories, reviews and news reportage to Comic Book Marketplace, Cinefantastique/CFQ, International Studio, Sketch, Tripwire and various other genre magazines. During the same period, Bill also served as a columnist and reporter for a number of websites, including www.ComicBookResources.com and www.WizardWorld.com. These days, when he's not working on his latest interview, article or book, Bill serves as the host of "Baker's Dozen," a periodic column of short but meaty interviews with comic book creators, game designers and other purveyors of Pop Culture, for www.WorldFamousComics.com.

Bill currently resides in the wilds of the Upper Peninsula of Michigan, where he's preparing the next volume in the "Bill Baker Presents..." series [George Perez: The Best of All Worlds] and a second edition of Alan Moore Spells It Out. Heartened by the positive response to the original short story he contributed to the recently released Wicked West 2 anthology (Image, 2006), Bill's begun work on several of his own creative projects.

You can learn more about what Bill Baker's been working on and thinking about of late by visiting his blog, Speculative Friction, at http://specfric.blogspot.com. And you'll find more information concerning Bill's career and past work on his professional website, www.BloodintheGutters.com.